First World War
and Army of Occupation
War Diary
France, Belgium and Germany

24 DIVISION
Headquarters, Branches and Services
Royal Army Ordnance Corps
Assistant Director Ordnance Services
21 August 1915 - 31 December 1918

WO95/2196/3

The Naval & Military Press Ltd
www.nmarchive.com
Published in association with The National Archives

Published by

The Naval & Military Press Ltd

Unit 10 Ridgewood Industrial Park,

Uckfield, East Sussex,

TN22 5QE England

Tel: +44 (0) 1825 749494

www.naval-military-press.com

www.nmarchive.com

This diary has been reprinted in facsimile from the original. Any imperfections are inevitably reproduced and the quality may fall short of modern type and cartographic standards.

© **Crown Copyright**
Images reproduced by permission of The National Archives, London, England, 2015.

Contents

Document type	Place/Title	Date From	Date To
Miscellaneous	WO95/2196-3		
Heading	Dep Asst Dir. Ordnance Services Aug 1915-Dec 1918		
Heading	H.Q. 24th Div. D.A.D.S. Vol I. Aug To Oct 15 Dec 18		
Heading	War Diary Of D.A.D.O.S. 24th Division from 21st August 1915 to 20th October 1915		
War Diary	Blackdown	21/08/1915	24/08/1915
War Diary	Folkestone	25/08/1915	25/08/1915
War Diary	Boulogne	26/08/1915	26/08/1915
War Diary	Montreuil	27/08/1915	31/08/1915
War Diary	Royon	01/09/1915	23/09/1915
War Diary	Busnes	24/09/1915	25/09/1915
War Diary	Bethune	26/09/1915	26/09/1915
War Diary	Sailly Labourse	27/09/1915	30/09/1915
War Diary	St. Hiliars	01/10/1915	02/10/1915
War Diary	Steenwoorde	03/10/1915	06/10/1915
War Diary	Renninghelst	07/10/1915	20/10/1915
Heading	H.Q. 24th Div. D.A.D.O.S. Vol 2 Nov 15		
Heading	War Diary Of D.A.D.O.S. 24th Division From 1st November 1915 To 30th November 1915		
War Diary	Aire	01/11/1915	08/11/1915
War Diary	Reninghelst	08/11/1915	20/11/1915
War Diary	Moulle	21/11/1915	29/11/1915
Heading	D.A.D.O.S. 24th Div. Vol. 3		
War Diary	Moulle	15/12/1915	31/12/1915
Heading	D.A.D.O.S. 24th Div. Vol. 4 Jan		
War Diary	Moulle	01/01/1916	04/01/1916
War Diary	Reninghelst	05/01/1916	31/01/1916
Heading	D.A.D.O.S. 24th Div. Vol. 5		
War Diary	Reninghelst	01/02/1916	29/02/1916
Heading	D.A.D.O.S. 24th Div. Vol. 6		
War Diary	Reninghelst	01/03/1916	20/03/1916
War Diary	Fletre	21/03/1916	28/03/1916
War Diary	Baillieul	29/03/1916	30/04/1916
Miscellaneous	D.A.G. 3rd Echelon	04/06/1916	04/06/1916
War Diary	Bailleul	01/05/1916	31/07/1916
Miscellaneous	D.A.A. & Q.M.S. 24th Div.	02/09/1916	02/09/1916
War Diary	Corbie	01/08/1916	03/08/1916
War Diary	Morlancourt	03/08/1916	03/08/1916
War Diary	Filiform Tree	04/08/1916	31/08/1916
Miscellaneous	D.A.D.O.S.	26/08/1916	26/08/1916
War Diary	Albert Sheet 62D E I Central	01/09/1916	07/09/1916
War Diary	Ailly Le Haut Clocher	08/09/1916	19/09/1916
War Diary	Bruay	20/09/1916	23/09/1916
War Diary	Estre Cauchie	24/09/1916	30/09/1916
Miscellaneous	D.A.G. 3rd Echelon	26/12/1916	26/12/1916
War Diary	Estre Cauchy	01/10/1916	31/10/1916
War Diary	Bracquemont	01/11/1916	31/12/1916
War Diary	Braquemont	01/01/1917	31/01/1917
War Diary	Bracquemont	01/02/1917	12/02/1917
War Diary	Labeuvriere	13/02/1917	04/03/1917

War Diary	Noeux Les Mines	05/03/1917	21/04/1917
War Diary	Fontes	22/04/1917	15/05/1917
War Diary	Poperinge G 14 6 Central (Map 28)	16/05/1917	24/05/1917
War Diary	G 14 b central Map 26 (Nr Poperinge)	25/05/1917	31/05/1917
Heading	War Diary Lieut A.F. Dodds. A.O.D. From 10/6/1917 To 30/6/1917 Vol 21		
Miscellaneous	To Be Forwarded To D.A.A.G. 24 Div By The 7th Of The Month Following		
Miscellaneous	D.A.A.G. 24th Division	30/06/1917	30/06/1917
War Diary	Sheet 28 G.26.C. Central	01/06/1917	09/06/1917
War Diary	Renninghelst (Sheet 27 G. 32. C. 5.4)	10/06/1917	12/06/1917
War Diary	Sheet 28. N.1. Central	13/06/1917	27/06/1917
War Diary	Lumbres	28/06/1917	30/06/1917
Miscellaneous	D.A.G. 3rd Echelon	11/08/1917	11/08/1917
War Diary	Lumbres	01/07/1917	21/07/1917
War Diary	Reninghelst	22/07/1917	31/07/1917
War Diary	G 35 b 4.9 Reninghelst Ouderdom Road	01/08/1917	11/08/1917
War Diary	G 35 b 4.9.	12/08/1917	28/08/1917
Heading	D.A.D.O.S. 24 Div. Vol 24		
War Diary	G35 b 4.9 Reninghelst Ouderdom Road	01/09/1917	15/09/1917
War Diary	Merris	16/09/1917	19/09/1917
War Diary	Beugny Haplincourt Road	20/09/1917	28/09/1917
War Diary	Nobescourt Farm	29/09/1917	30/09/1917
Miscellaneous	D.A.G. Office. Base		
War Diary	Nobescourt Farm	01/10/1917	18/10/1917
War Diary	K 31 Central Map 62C	19/10/1917	31/10/1917
Miscellaneous	D.A.G. 3rd Echelon Base	01/12/1917	01/12/1917
War Diary	Nobescourt Farm K 33 Central Map 62C	01/11/1917	30/11/1917
Miscellaneous	D.A.G., 3rd Echelon Base.		
War Diary	Nobescourt Farm K 33 Central 62 C Map	01/12/1917	31/12/1917
Miscellaneous	D.A.G., Third Echelon.	23/06/1918	23/06/1918
War Diary	Nobescourt Farm K 33 Central 62C (Map)	01/01/1918	04/03/1918
War Diary	Flamicourt (Peronne)	05/03/1918	15/03/1918
War Diary	Bouvincourt	16/03/1918	21/03/1918
War Diary	Brie	22/03/1918	24/03/1918
War Diary	Roziers	25/03/1918	25/03/1918
War Diary	Demuin	26/03/1918	27/03/1918
War Diary	Castel	28/03/1918	28/03/1918
War Diary	Cottenchy	29/03/1918	31/03/1918
Miscellaneous	D.A.G. 3rd Echelon.	26/06/1918	26/06/1918
War Diary	Cottenchy	01/04/1918	03/04/1918
War Diary	Boves	04/04/1918	04/04/1918
War Diary	Boutillerie	05/04/1918	05/04/1918
War Diary	St Valery	06/04/1918	17/04/1918
War Diary	La Thieuloye	17/04/1918	03/05/1918
War Diary	Boyeffles	04/05/1918	08/05/1918
War Diary	Gouy Servins	09/05/1918	31/05/1918
War Diary	Gouy Servins W 5 Central Map 44 b	09/05/1918	28/06/1918
War Diary	Gouy Servins	29/06/1918	30/06/1918
Miscellaneous	D.A.A.G. 24th Division		
War Diary		01/07/1918	06/07/1918
War Diary	Gouyservins	07/07/1918	14/07/1918
War Diary	Boyeffles	15/07/1918	30/09/1918
War Diary	Lucheux	01/10/1918	01/10/1918
War Diary	Moevres	06/10/1918	08/10/1918
War Diary	Fontaine Notre Dames	09/10/1918	12/10/1918

War Diary	B. 20.b. (51A)	13/10/1918	16/10/1918
War Diary	Avesnes Les Aubert	17/10/1918	21/10/1918
War Diary	Cambrai	22/10/1918	26/10/1918
War Diary	St Aubert	27/10/1918	02/11/1918
War Diary	Bermerain	03/11/1918	04/11/1918
War Diary	Warnies Le Grand	05/11/1918	09/11/1918
War Diary	Bavay	10/11/1918	18/11/1918
War Diary	Tournai	23/12/1918	31/12/1918

00995/2196/3

24TH DIVISION
DIVL TROOPS

DEP ASST DIR. ORDNANCE SERVICES

AUG 1915 – DEC 1918

24TH DIVISION
DIVL TROOPS

121/7608

24th Kurum

No. 20 S Sri. SNOO.

Vol I

Aug to Oct. 15

Dec '15

Confidential

War Diary

D.A.D.O.S. of 24th Division

From 21st August 1915. To 20th October 1915

Army Form C. 2118.

WAR DIARY
or
INTELLIGENCE SUMMARY.
(Erase heading not required.)

Instructions regarding War Diaries and Intelligence Summaries are contained in F.S. Regs., Part II. and the Staff Manual respectively. Title pages will be prepared in manuscript.

Place	Date	Hour	Summary of Events and Information	Remarks and references to Appendices
			The 24th Division 3rd New Army was formed at Shoreham Sussex on the 11th Sept 1914 and ordered to be Equipped to Mobilization Scale (A. form G. 1098 Series) 1st May 1915. The Division moved to Blackdown & ordered (for Completion of Equipt & Final training) by road & march route June 1st 15. Instructions were received to Mobilize on 21st August 1915 and to proceed overseas.	
Blackdown	21/8/15		Drawing Stores to Complete A.O.S.	
"	22/8/15		Drawing Stores to Complete A.O.S.	
"	23/8/15		Rations & Ammunl. Col. drew Sm. Arms & all units drew extra draw Smoke Helmets.	
"	24/8/15	4.Bn.	Received instructions to proceed to France via Folkestone & Boulogne.	
"	--	4.35pm	Left Blackdown. arrived Sandgate 9 P.m. With Motor Car, Buses & Servants. Put up for the night.	
Folkestone	25/8/15	8.30am	Arrived Folkestone Harbour. Embarked Motor 3 Pm & Sailed for Boulogne 4-20 Pm. Arrived 6 Pm. & reported to Base Commandant; remained at Boulogne for night.	
Boulogne	26/8/15	9 am	Started for Abbeville by Motor Car. arrived 11.15 am. reported to H.Q.2 & D.O.S. Endeavoured to find suitable to await arrival of Division.	
Montreuil	27/8/15		Started R. O. Depot B/Staples	
"	28/8/15		Started Head Qrs. Billet of 24 Dn: Rouen. & arranged for Officer accommodation.	
"	28/8/15		To Boulogne for Stationery Practical R.O.D. Spect. thence to Abbeville, re Smoke Helmets.	

Army Form C. 2118.

WAR DIARY
or
INTELLIGENCE SUMMARY.
(Erase heading not required.)

Instructions regarding War Diaries and Intelligence Summaries are contained in F.S. Regs., Part II. and the Staff Manual respectively. Title pages will be prepared in manuscript.

Place	Date	Hour	Summary of Events and Information	Remarks and references to Appendices
Monchaud	29/8/15		Visited No. 2 Qr Abbeville to arrange motor lorries in respect to P. Spiers & Pads. Smith Helmets.	
-"-	30/8/15		for M.nero & latest pattern Smoke Helmets.	
-"-	31/8/15		Took particulars of Specifers, mixing of Solution most made up of Respirators with locality. Head Qr. 24 Division Arrived Royon--	

2353 Wt. W2514/1434 700,000 5/15 D.D. & L.   A.D.S.S./Forms/C. 2118.

Army Form C. 2118.

WAR DIARY
or
INTELLIGENCE SUMMARY.
(Erase heading not required.)

Place	Date	Hour	Summary of Events and Information	Remarks and references to Appendices
Rouen	1- 9/15	2. P.M	Removed from Montreuil to Rouen. Visited Beauvainville Railway Station (Railhead)	
-"-	2- 9/15		Visited trains.	
-"-	3- 9/15		Nothing exceptional to note.	
-"-	4- 9/15		Colonel Green A.D.M.S XI Corps called in reference to transport of sick	
-"-	5- 9/15		To St Omer W.K D.A.Q.M.G 24 Div. Called on A.D.O.S. H.Q Qrs.	
-"-	6- 9/15		Visited 24 Div. Ammt Column in reference to Small Arm Ammnt, T.I.B Pen Q.F. Shell, Also Sect Park.	
-"-	7- 9/15		To St Omer received instructions regarding Smoke Helmets	
-"-	8- 9/15		To Railway Station Beauvainville 8 Lewis Machine Guns rec'd in Div. G.O.C XI Corps inspected Park	
-"-	9- 9/15		of Arts went to Abbeville re issues of Gas Helmets & Respirators to be held -	
-"-	10- 9/15 11- 9/15		Nothing exceptional to note	
-"-	12- 9/15		To Beauvainville Ry Station rec'd Stores & Stationery for distr. also Stepney Machine Guns to complete	
-"-	13- 9/15		Rec'd Quick Stores & removed to Depôts	
-"-	14- 9/15		Do. Do. Do.	
-"-	15- 9/16		Do. Do. Do.	

Army Form C. 2118.

WAR DIARY
or
INTELLIGENCE SUMMARY.
(Erase heading not required.)

Instructions regarding War Diaries and Intelligence Summaries are contained in F. S. Regs., Part II. and the Staff Manual respectively. Title pages will be prepared in manuscript.

Place	Date	Hour	Summary of Events and Information	Remarks and references to Appendices
Rouen	16. 9/15		To Beauranville Ry Station, & arranged to store Rounds of Respirators.	
-"-	17. 9/15		D° with A.A.T.Q.M.G.2nd Army. thence to Sub Park in reference to receipt of Grenades etc.	
-"-	18. 9/15	9 am	D° Rec'd Lyp Drenching Machine for H.Q. 24 Div. and other stores.	
-"-	19. 9/15		Nothing of interest to note	
-"-	20. 9/15		To Rouen. Re Ammn for Sub Park.	
-"-	21. 9/15		Arranged Park Inspection & took Spadroot to Lillers. 24 S.A.A. moved to B'Busnes. 6 Pm. Godstep arrives to Complete	
-"-	22. 9/15		Received 1000 Blankets left in Park by 71st Bde. put them on Rail & despatch to Lillers.	
-"-	23. 9/15	8.30 a	A.D.Syt left for Amiens. with 4 motor Lorries. Companies all Blanket to Bruay Park.	
Amiens	24. 9/15		Received 550 Bomb Carriers from O.O. XI Corps. received 50 6 each of the 13 Bns. in the Division	
-"-	-"-		Received 7400 Smoke Helmets with tubes from St Omer & issued to A.D.S also issued 300 Smoke Helmets to men 2 R.F.A.	
-"-	-"-		Returned 51 Cases (1200) Respirators to Base Park. Division moves to Ruchew en Rouhy. Vermelles.	
-"-	25. 9/15	9 am	Started for rate the A.D.Syt. & 11 Lorries & Stores arrived Bethune 10.30 pm	
Bethune	26. 9/15	8 am	Started for Sailly Labourse & sent 2 Lorries to St Omer for Gas Like Helmets. Received 300 Leather 7 Sheepshin	
Sailly Labourse	27. 9/15		Coats Skin Coats to Field Ambulances, 100 to each.	
-"-	28. 9/15		Issued all Coats received from Park.	
-"-	29. 9/15	8 am	Moved to S.E. Hilaire. Completed H.Q. 24 Div. Issue of 1 Blanket per man.	
-"-	30. 9/15		Issued all Stores received from Park.	

Army Form C. 2118.

WAR DIARY
or
INTELLIGENCE SUMMARY.
(Erase heading not required.)

Instructions regarding War Diaries and Intelligence Summaries are contained in F.S. Regs., Part II. and the Staff Manual respectively. Title pages will be prepared in manuscript.

Place	Date	Hour	Summary of Events and Information	Remarks and references to Appendices
St Nilino	1- 10/10		Issued Stores to recognite Bn.	
-"-	2. 10/15	12 noon	Left for Stavoroške —	
Stavoroške	3. 10/10		To Granite Railway Station (Radhast) Rec'd S.R. Truck of Stores arrived & truck at Stavoroške ADOS 2nd Army/Baltic Division. Sent 2 lories to unload & 3. Other to unload of Garibaldi Completion men of stores 5 Division as far as possible, including 14 Lewis Part Magazines Guns to 71st Bde	
-"-	4. 10/15		Returned 50 Pair Respirators (2000) to 3rd Base Hosp T. Inspected armt of Staro 11 Bn.	
-"-	5. 10/15		Received & issued G.S. Wagons Water Cart T Kindling Section to unit of Divi also Infant Assembly T7 Mountain Guns	
-"-	6. 10/15		Removed to Birminghilok, near Radhost, near [crossed out] Podewaroffee	
Birminghilok	7. 10/15		Received 1 Hackney Rotation 2 Handcart Wagon 1 GS Wagon 1 Lorrie 18 Prs. 1 Water Cart Trainsend 2- horses ADOS 2nd Army Baltic	
-"-	8. 10/15		Blankets & Waterproof sheets received, issued forwarding —	
-"-	9. 10/15		Army Patrol Stores trans arriving regularly	
-"-	10. 10/15		Nothing exceptional to note	
-"-	11-10/15		Do	
-"-	12. 10/15		Do	
-"-	13. 10/15		Received 250 Magazines for Lewis Machine Guns invoiced, for distribution to each Bde of Div. 71st Bde Radio transport to 6th Mon 17th Bde/Bde trans 24 AM	
-"-	14. 10/15		Received from 5th Corps 135 Pair Mined Boots (various sizes) invoiced 1-72 & 73 Whigh Return Magazines boots & I om Wrack in report. Issue of BMK T medical stores progressing	
-"-	15. 10/15		Do	
-"-	16. 10/15		Do	
-"-	17. 10/15		Received Magazines for Machine Guns to complete Div.	
-"-	18. 10/15		BM&T Medical Stores received T issued —	
-"-	19. 10/15		Do Capt R.S. Karwick arrived as my relief AD a MS	
-"-	20. 10/15		Left Division in Route for England	

2353 Wt. W2541/1454 700,000 5/15 B.D. & L. S.A.D.S.S./Forms/C. 2118.

126/7605

H.O. 24th Str:
S.A.O.S.
vol 2

Nov. 15

Confidential

War Diary

of

D.A.D.O.S. 24th Division

from 1st November 1915 to 30 same month.

Army Form C. 2118.

DOO 2nd Cav Divn

WAR DIARY
or
INTELLIGENCE SUMMARY.
(Erase heading not required.)

Instructions regarding War Diaries and Intelligence Summaries are contained in F. S. Regs., Part II. and the Staff Manual respectively. Title pages will be prepared in manuscript.

Place	Date	Hour	Summary of Events and Information	Remarks and references to Appendices
AIRE	Nov 1-8		Divn. settling down in billets between railhead AIRE, Hd Qrs 5th Cav Bde at PARENTY. Hd Qrs of Divn at THIEMBRONNE. 2nd Pol Squadron R.E. at LE NIEPPE superintending digging trenches. 1500 gumboots thigh were issued for this purpose, withdrawn & replaced by boots F.S. when it was pointed out that the rubber boot would be useless for digging.	

O Bulfin Major General
DOO 2nd

WAR DIARY
INTELLIGENCE SUMMARY.

ADS 2nd Div.

Army Form C. 2118

Place	Date	Hour	Summary of Events and Information	Remarks and references to Appendices
RENINGHELST	Nov 8		Posted 2/c "Div" on 5 Nov vice John(?) as DADOS on 8th Nov. Took over Div from	C
			Capt J.S. Kenrick 10D who left on 9/15. The Div is a new from Div. - has been practically reorganised since the attack at Loos, is now in the trenches. Being new army they require a certain amount of looking after but they are coming into him. The place is very dark, naturally. Stores come up regularly. The AOD staff are good. The 4 AOD lorries and from the Base to GODWEARSVELDE. An unloaded wb(?) the 4 AOD lorries and thought to depot at RENINGHELST, units as a rule come first thou next day.	C
	12.		A very large supply of lead billions have been received from DUNKIRK and are now a day in the market. They are gradually been expended. An armoury shop has been started with three armourers for repair of rifles, bicycles. Tools have been indented for. I am not yet certain as to the advantages of having a Div't shop. but I hear that some of the armourers an trying and more so Cant Q.M.S's than at their proper work.	C
	17.		Head Div was moving one of the trenches to Wear of St. Omer. Instead on the 26th"	C
	18.		Wired to Param to stop issues. Units will not accept when on the move.	C
	19.		Just Subject of how cage getting aout. food rocks in possessions	C

Army Form C. 2118.

WAR DIARY
or
INTELLIGENCE SUMMARY.

(Erase heading not required.)

Instructions regarding War Diaries and Intelligence Summaries are contained in F. S. Regs., Part II. and the Staff Manual respectively. Title pages will be prepared in manuscript.

Place	Date	Hour	Summary of Events and Information	Remarks and references to Appendices
RENINGHELST	Nov. 20		Jo. visited new railhead at WATTEN. went and found depot & office at MOULLE.	2
MOULLE	21st		Moved old depot to Moulle. in 2 lorries. Handed over great quantity of stores, including French stoves to 3rd Divl. Stores on 18000 small helmets at Steenwoorde. All units generally overloaded with kit. both new units. Am finding some difficulty in getting first rain cars to unit.	S1
	22nd		Jo-Cyrop to find out when new railhead starts. not begun 23rd.	S1
	23rd		Jo-Calais made arrangements for 2 Dn AOD stores to arrive WATTEN tomorrow.	S1
	24th		First arrival of stores at new railhead.	S1
	25		Lt. J.H.O. Sheppard arrived today from Havre to for instruction. Authority received today for 2nd blanket, 2nd Gds helmet, + steel helmet for all Svc.	S1
	26		II Army dy Mot Workshop to distribute stores to units & reserve transport, have made arrangements about repair of vehicles.	S1
	26		got wounded men in to distribute stores to all units outside & no railway from here. 1	S1
			arrangements to distribute by lorry to all units. 1 Regt. 1 comple. Ren. 1 Bde RFA DAC. only comes to	S1
	27		5 trucks in - am getting a great quantity of stores, but units are coming in tomorrow, 1, 2 Ambulances are harrying away a good deal.	S1
			The weather for last 10 days of month has been very cold. Seven from adverse in with rain.	S1

O. W. Cole. Major
DDD. 2d Dn

Stapo. 24/1. Stapi.
Bd: 3

13/
7910

Army Form C. 2118.

WAR DIARY
or
INTELLIGENCE SUMMARY.
(Erase heading not required.)

Instructions regarding War Diaries and Intelligence Summaries are contained in F.S. Regs., Part II. and the Staff Manual respectively. Title pages will be prepared in manuscript.

Place	Date	Hour	Summary of Events and Information	Remarks and references to Appendices
MOULLE	Dec 1915 15		Major Iredale posted to 20th Division for temporary duty as D.A.D.O.S.	JMcN
	16			
	17		Left as acting D.A.D.O.S. Major W.C. Iredale left this morning. Twenty Lewis Machine Guns up from the Base for issue to five old force battalions of the division who are in possession of Vickers or Maxim Guns. This being done to finally release the Vickers etc. thus enabling them to be used in the formation of the first Machine Gun Company now being formed. This to be done when units are trained in the use of the Lewis Gun.	J.A.S.
	22		Went to inspect new refilling point at Poperinghe, which we are taking over from the 14th Division. The store itself is good. I understand one of the best of all. Part of the roof has lately been partially damaged owing to shell fire. A man was left there to acquaint himself formally to take over the stores from the 14th Division. Capt Beckwith is the D.A.D.O.S.	JMcS
	23		Went to inspect a temporary stores which the A.A.&Q.M.G. has taken at WATTEN close to the Railway Station. As it is not yet certain whether this area is to be a permanent rest area. It has been arranged to place all stores not required in the new area in this building instead of sending them back to the Base. These stores which units find they want later will then also be available from this place, as each unit is having a portion allotted for their stores. It cannot take up at the time of the move. All units should be fully re-equipped. Very large demands	

WAR DIARY
INTELLIGENCE SUMMARY
(Erase heading not required.)

Army Form C. 2118.

Place	Date	Hour	Summary of Events and Information	Remarks and references to Appendices
MOULLE	Dec 1915			
	24		in most stores have been met. The weather mild & generally a good deal of rain. Went to Poperinghe to make the final arrangements before taking over new store. Saw the Convent at St Sixtes where an advance expected to go, then held by 49th Division also went to the Ordnance refilling point for the same division, which was about 1 mile away from the @ Officio. Called in at the town Major's office on the way back thro' Poperinghe to fix up what office accommodation Follett might be requiring. Arranged with D.O.O. 4th Division to let me start sending up my issues of talc smoke helmets.	J.M.D.
	25		Xmas Day. A quiet day on the whole. In the afternoon the Staff were given the rest of the day off. Leaving only enough people to look after the stores & to be able to issue anything if required. The men had a gathering in an adjoining school, music etc. Had a wire from D.O.O. 14th Div in the evening to say they were returning their refilling point in Poperinghe.	J.M.D.
	26		Rang up 'Q' on the telephone to find out what was happening. Was told then that the move had been postponed. Everything then has to be cancelled & simply continue as before but always feeling that it might be necessary to move at any time.	J.M.D.
	27		Nothing further known about the move, hence rather a difficulty in keeping the stores in the refilling point down to a minimum.	
	28		Great difficulty in obtaining sufficient nose-bags. Went to Merville & ordered 200, expect to have to get more as 600 are due from base supplies are below demand each week in this item. A very interesting article to the British manufactured bag is only obtainable at an increased cost. Great sums of money are thus spent, which by the production at home, would be saved. It is all female labour & surely the material could be obtained.	J.M.D.

Army Form C. 2118.

WAR DIARY
or
INTELLIGENCE SUMMARY.

(Erase heading not required.)

Instructions regarding War Diaries and Intelligence Summaries are contained in F. S. Regs., Part II. and the Staff Manual respectively. Title pages will be prepared in manuscript.

Place	Date	Hour	Summary of Events and Information	Remarks and references to Appendices
MOULLE	December/15			
	29		Heard the division is to relieve the 17th division shortly. Went thro' to RENINGHELST to see the refilling point which we are to take over. It is situated about a mile from Reninghelst off the road into Poppringhe. Appears to be a very poor show as nothing can be locked up & so much has to be even left outside under tarpaulins. Obtained authority to purchase 600 metwraps. These to include the 200 ordered yesterday. JMD.	
	30		Lt. Weller A.O.D. came here from 17th Division to inspect this refilling point. I took him out & rather to see the Divisional Store Men. It has only been started a week & was very full of stores - JMD.	
	31		To RENINGHELST to find out billeting accommodation for men etc, went to 'Q' office in that town used by 17th Division. Took D. Warrant Officer with me to see the new site. JMD.	

J.M.D. Dickinson
Lt. D.S.O. 24th Division

Army Form C. 2118.

WAR DIARY
or
INTELLIGENCE SUMMARY.
(Erase heading not required.)

Instructions regarding War Diaries and Intelligence Summaries are contained in F.S. Regs., Part II and the Staff Manual respectively. Title pages will be prepared in manuscript.

Place	Date	Hour	Summary of Events and Information	Remarks and references to Appendices
MOULLE	1st January -16		21 Steel Helmets had to be withdrawn from the 3 Brigade to enable the R.E. (Signals) to have this number. They do not at present get them, but these were voted by special instructions from the S.O.C.	J.H.D.
	2nd		As the 20 New Lewis guns recently issued had only 12 magazines each instead of 64, the S.O.C. decided to withdraw 18 from each of the remaining 9 battalions. These were split up over the 20 guns thus leaves them each with 44 magazines while the 9 O/S now have 46 per gun.	J.H.D.
	3rd		Artillery units beginning to move - stopped all detail stores for these units	J.H.D.
	4th		Handed over 19500 tube helmets to the 17th Division, who also took over some tarpaulin trails - Twenty E.P. Tents which were lent to the division whilst at rest were all returned to No 12 Casualty Clearing Station HAZEBROUCK, the first lot being sent on this day -	
REMINGHELST	5		Took over the 17th Divisional Ordnance Store, which is slightly out of the area, but altho' a bad store in some ways, it is hoped to be able to retain. Some 400 tons of stone being put down by 17th Divn. the entrance that are quite good for lorry use. It is an old farm house, the position on the map is Sheet 28 (B Series) G.27 x 5.8 19500 (3rd reserve) smoke helmets taken over, also a few trench stores including 1161 Boots from Thigh.	

CONT?

WAR DIARY
or
INTELLIGENCE SUMMARY.
(Erase heading not required.)

Army Form C. 2118.

Place	Date	Hour	Summary of Events and Information	Remarks and references to Appendices
RENINGHELST	5th Dec		Went to GODEWAERSVELDE to find out when our railhead would be there. Found that not until 8th Jan. could this railhead be used + for the present time ARNEKE has to be used. This is approx: two hours & half's run. Means very long hours for the few lorries.	
	6th		Beginning to settle down in new store. Went to Estaires & Merville to buy British cloths, nose bags & bread carriers. Brought back 1000 of the former, the first of 10,000 consignment. 400 nose bags & 200 bread carriers.	
	7th		It is thought that possibly the "Q" +"S" quarters will be moved to the Convent in POPERINGHE instead of RENINGHELST. The Divisional Technical School being now in the Convent. The "Q" office to be established tomorrow. The weather is very windy + certain amount of rain.	J.M.D.
	8th		To GODEWAERSVELDE to find stores would not be coming up to that railhead before the 9th of the month, still sending lorries to ARNEKE. Stores coming up from there alright but a tremendous journey for the lorries.	J.M.D.
	9th		To Audruicq to buy Lumber Hooks, great difficulty in obtaining these from the Base. Units beginning to come in for stores.	J.M.D.
	10th		Went to GODEWAERSVELDE to find railhead was not to be changed from ARNEKE. First issue of stores from the new railhead GODEWAERSVELDE. This making a great deal of difference to the lorries, as now it is quite possible to assist the Salvage Dump & get their stores in a dry condition to Dunkerque. Went to DUNKERQUE to place order for a Special lorry requires for taking men's socks up to units.	J.M.D.

Army Form C. 2118.

WAR DIARY
or
INTELLIGENCE SUMMARY.
(Erase heading not required.)

Instructions regarding War Diaries and Intelligence Summaries are contained in F. S. Regs., Part II. and the Staff Manual respectively. Title pages will be prepared in manuscript.

Place	Date	Hour	Summary of Events and Information	Remarks and references to Appendices
	11.1.16		A man, instructed in the repair of gum boots, reported here to instruct 6 other men sent in from the Brigades in the patching of these stores with a view to these men being able to meet all the small repairs for the division. It has been decided that 3 men will be sufficient to keep employed on this work for the present.	J.H.O.
	12.1.16		The Salvage Dump is 3¾ mile away. One lorry is sent each day, after finishing incoming stores from railhead, to clear stores for railhead from this store. It brings them to this store where they are looked over & those required for the service retained. The balance goes up to railhead in the morning in the otherwise empty lorries going to railhead.	J.H.O.
	13.1.16		To Estaires to bring back 2800 breech covers (local purchase). Ordered 150 mactrops. These items still coming up very much under demands - only 50% met.	J.H.O.
	14.1.16		To Dunkerque to get socks bags - 167 obtained out of the order for 300 -. Car broken down - now in the Divisional Supply Col. shops. Small chance of being repaired under 2 or 3 weeks. Very difficult to get about to do necessary work.	J.H.O.
		1000	Tube Helmets received from the Corps to meet unforeseen - these stores coming up short from only 25% of outstanding demands being met. Colonel Bush came to inspect stores from V Corps today.	J.H.O.
	15.1.16		To Bailleul to buy hurricane lamps; 17th Div seem to have left practically nothing behind, all our hurricane lamps left in vet area to units practically none in new area.	J.H.O.
	16.1.16		Still great shortage of nose bags - only 33% coming up from base. Authority obtained to buy 1026 from II Army - Brigade Machine Gun Company formed from 17th Brigade.	J.H.O.
	17.1.16		To DUNKERQUE to fetch remainder of sock bags for Divisional Baths - also ordered 50 of new sort of funnels for R. carrier - these required by GOC. as at last lot.	J.H.O.
	18.1.16		To ESTAIRES for 3200 breech covers, also got six limber hooks from V Corps Workshop out of 40 bought & took them to be drilled.	J.H.O.

WAR DIARY
INTELLIGENCE SUMMARY

Army Form C. 2118.

Place	Date	Hour	Summary of Events and Information	Remarks and references to Appendices
RENINGHELST	19.1.16		(Continued)	
		20-	Trench cards received - A very doubtful & uncertain statement as reports from Corps on certain items contained therein (e.g. Gum boots) differ by thousands.	
		21-	A.D.O.S. I Corps came to visit the store. Paid a surprise visit to Q.M.S. Stores (13th Moorloos) found far too many stores being held up there. Unit's reply is "I've just drawn this from Ordnance" they are nearly all being visited tomorrow. Formed out to unit that from the point of view of mobility, reserves in case of a sudden move such large stocks must not be held.	J.H.D. J.H.D.
		22-	To Mons des Cats to take 5 Telescopic rifles to School of Snipping - Instr. instructions from D.D.P. II Army all these rifles now received for the division are to first go to this place. To BAILLIEUL to get divisional demands for these items for local purchase. To MERVILLE for 1000 Nose bags. To HAZEBROUCK to try to obtain trench carts for 9 of Battalions in Division at rate of 4 per Batt: G.O.C. very anxious to obtain these. Finis II Army R.E. workshops at HAZEBROUCK the only place these can be obtained. They must be requisitioned by R.E. K's. To I Corps workshops STEENVOORDE to get timber hooks which I purchased & required drilling, as this was not possible at the foundry where they were obtained.	J.H.D. J.H.D. J.H.D.
		23-	To DUNKERQUE to get a new pattern model of tent carrier, which the G.O.C. has decided to try 50 of.	J.H.D.
		24.	To BAILLIEUL & ARMENTIÈRES for local purchase - Bought 200 mugs from coffee pots for a new Coffee House the Fort is opening. Received the surplus 4 Machine Guns from B.M. Gun Officer for return to Base.	J.H.D.

Army Form C. 2118.

WAR DIARY
or
INTELLIGENCE SUMMARY.

(Erase heading not required.)   (Continued.)

Place	Date	Hour	Summary of Events and Information	Remarks and references to Appendices
RENINGHELST	25.1.16		Orders received to return all old pattern (divisional reserve) hypo smoke helmets to the base having received 5000 Tube pattern to be held as Divisional Reserve	JHD
	26.		20,400 Hypo sponge pattern helmets returned to base. Another sponge pattern helmet for the use of Artillery at the rate of 24 pr battery received. This is necessary due to the fact that to prevent any ill results to the eyes it is necessary to wear both the anti gas goggles & the helmet. The two glasses make it impossible for the gunners to read their sights & hence the necessity for a tube helmet which can keep the explosive shell gas from the eyes.	JHD
	27		Instructions received that a further pattern of Tube helmet called P.H. is to be issued & to every officer & man in the division. Them release by this issue to be returned to the Base, as soon as possible to withdraw from units.	JHD
	28		Now hear it is finally intended to personally issue 2 new P.H. Tube helmets to the officers & men of the division. A demand submitted to the base for the 2nd helmet up to Strength of the Division	JHD
	29		To AUDRUICQ to try & place an order for some trench carts. The division is in great need of these, which I understand is really an R.E. service & made at R.E. II Army Workshops HAZEBROUCK. Spoke to CRE who said he could only get very small quantities & would like me to try to obtain also.	JHD
	30		Lorry taken by the Supply Column - not for repair purposes, but presumably owing to shortage on the column.	JHD
	31		To railhead where everything seemed quite satisfactory. A fresh man allotted for railhead work on the lorries in the absence of the usual man who has gone on leave.	JHD

J.H.D. Sheppard Lt. D.S.O. 24th Division

D.A.D.O.S.
24th Div
Vol. 5

Army Form C. 2118.

WAR DIARY
or
INTELLIGENCE SUMMARY.
(Erase heading not required.)

Instructions regarding War Diaries and Intelligence Summaries are contained in F. S. Regs., Part II. and the Staff Manual respectively. Title pages will be prepared in manuscript.

Place	Date	Hour	Summary of Events and Information	Remarks and references to Appendices
RENINGHELST	1st Feb 16		Instructions received to the effect that all Converted Maxims are to be replaced by Vickers Guns. There are 7 required in its Division, these are in possession of the 17th Brigade Machine Gun Company just recently formed.	G.H.Q.
	2		7 New Vickers Guns received from the Base. B.M.G. Officer notified to return his seven for exchange as soon as possible.	G.H.Q.
	3		4 Guns received from B.M.G. Officer 4.4 of the new ones issued. The old 4 despatched to the Base. Major Dudley now A.D.O.S. V Corps vice Lt Colonel Brush, he rang up today saying he was shortly coming down to inspect the store etc Remaining 3 Guns received from B.M.G. Officer of the 3 remaining New Vickers now issued. This completes the 7 Vickers so that now no C. Maxims remain in the division.	G.H.Q. G.H.Q.
	4			G.H.Q.
	5		Just supply of Lottery Lamp lights received for the Division, 14 in number. 3 Muzzle Pivoting machine Gun mountings received from A.S. Park under instructions from 5 Corps. This appears to be a new mounting but is not yet certain whether it is for use with Vickers or Lewis Guns.	G.H.Q.
	6		The Muzzle Pivoting Mounting can be used with either the Besides Maxim or the Lewis Gun with the aid of the adapter, however the Machine Gun sections are only to be in possession of same until the new Brigade Machine Gun companies are formed. The 17 Brigade M.G. Co. is the only one to date	G.H.Q.
	7		So Dunkirk for another sample of the boot carrier required by "S" Branch, so only to be had	G.H.Q.
	8		Gum boots beginning to come in large quantities for repairs, all the 6 new teams in	G.H.Q.

WAR DIARY
or
INTELLIGENCE SUMMARY.

Army Form C. 2118.

Place	Date	Hour	Summary of Events and Information	Remarks and references to Appendices
RENINGHELST	Feb. 8		This work had to be called in - The average output being only 4 to 5 pairs of boots per day	J.H.D.
	9		Fifty Bomb Carriers obtained from Dunkirque issued to Division	J.H.D.
	10 to 19		Sergt on leave. L/Cpl. of 17th Division doing duty for me - Arranged for 6 Armourers to go to L/Cpl workshop for instruction in Armourer Stores - Dist. Itinery found to be useful. Nose Bags now coming up regularly from the Base in full quantities	J.H.D.
	20		Great aerial activity, bombs dropped all round the neighbourhood, including one in the adjoining field to the store which exploded. Some of the men getting quite nervy thro' the continual bombing.	J.H.D.
	21			
	22		Weather turning very cold. a considerable amount of snow & frost	J.H.D.
	23		1 New Vickers gun received for the 17th B.M. Gun Co. to replace one damaged in action	J.H.D.
	24		2nd Issue of the new P.H. Tube Helmet all received up apparently all worried	J.H.D.
	25		C.R.E. wants 200 Stopping Slabs & the same number of Insulator wire for some special operations. Put the question up to Corps. Cutters were supplied thro' R.E. Parks, question of Stores hang on Base having great difficulties in meeting demand for these items.	J.H.D.
	26		Hears from Corps that 500 Sand Bags only are to be kept by R.E. Parks that 200 required by CRE are to be drawn from there	J.H.D.
	27		Thaw set in - Instructions that all traffic is to be kept down to a minimum. A "Jones respirator" is to be issued to Machine Gunners & Artillery men in lieu of Salinis Sets which are not to be replaces	J.H.D.

Army Form C. 2118.

WAR DIARY
or
INTELLIGENCE SUMMARY.
(Erase heading not required.)

Instructions regarding War Diaries and Intelligence Summaries are contained in F.S. Regs., Part II and the Staff Manual respectively. Title pages will be prepared in manuscript.

Place	Date	Hour	Summary of Events and Information	Remarks and references to Appendices
RENINGHELST	Feb 28		Thaw continues, traffic now reduces to a minimum on the roads. Rations brought up from Godewaersvelde to WIPPENHOEK f.H.D.	
	29		Railhead still in same place. Gumboot menders getting on faster with their repairs. Now averaging 6 pairs per man per day. Six men actually working on repairs, the remainder sorting, footing boots - Great stock of unserviceable boots to repair, some 450 pairs, these were all suddenly returned from units in a very bad state tracker floorboards the repair shop - f.H.D.	

J.H.D. Kerpan
Lt. D.90. 24th Division

Army Form C. 2118.

A.A.O.S 3
A 24 4A
Vol. 6

Army Form C. 2118.

WAR DIARY
or
INTELLIGENCE SUMMARY.
(Erase heading not required.)

Place	Date	Hour	Summary of Events and Information	Remarks and references to Appendices
RENINGHELST	1 March		Great difficulty in obtaining sufficient gum boot patches & especially Solution, thus keeping six men idle & some 500 pairs of unrepairable boots lying idle. Weather very severe, much enemy rifle grenages.	A.D.D.
	2		A special short rifle is required by 8 Branch for trench work, true with rifle grenades. They are 9 new incenerators in france. 2 have been tried by each Brigade for experiment.	A.D.D.
	3		Store bags are now coming up in full numbers. Approval received for a second satchel to carry P.H. helmet in place of patch pocket.	A.D.D.
	4		The Division complete with 2nd new P.H. Helmet. & 27,000 of the P type have already been returned to the Base.	A.D.D.
	5		200 Lewis Respirators out of 660 allotted to the Division have been received. These are in lieu finals of the Solina Breathing act. It is apparently expected of use over much longer periods. No replacements of Salvo sets are being made.	A.D.D.
	6		6" gun up at Railhead for the 6th Seige Battery.	A.D.D.
	7		To MERVILLE to obtain 74 shrouds required for observers in front. Corporal Bailey, an excellent clerk, orders to go to Grand Division - left today.	A.D.D.
	8		Run out of solution for gum boots again, altho demands thereland by air. A big number of outstanding boots true has to be put in after work. C. & Seige Battery to be administered as from Ordnance lorries going 5th Corps.	A.D.D.
	9		Heard from Base no gum boot solution in the country, arrives from home. Very heavy demands on the boots due to thaw of snow probably & apparently the end of life of most boots which were paired on new 2 months ago.	A.D.D.
	10		Am forme of 200 blankets made to C.R.E. for covering entrances to dug out etc to be storied with a special solution	A.D.D.

A.D.S.S. Forms/C. 2118.

WAR DIARY
INTELLIGENCE SUMMARY

Army Form C. 2118.

Place	Date	Hour	Summary of Events and Information	Remarks and references to Appendices
RENINGHELST	March 1916			
	11		To DUNKIRK to obtain special Swedish iron for making up some Strange Pesch plates, the present pattern being altogether too weak to withstand the strain.	JHD.
	12		Solution up for mending the Gum boots with at last expected of only enough supplies now to greatly increase the output of repaired boots. The Repair Shop having been enlarged while waiting for solution.	JHD.
	13		To BAILLEUL for syringes for C.R.E. to cow with special solution the new blankets issued for drafts & the 72nd Brigade Machine Gun Co. & 73rd Trench Mortar tyres. Many Small Stores required for them as this they have come out complete from home with guns tomplets turn out in England JHD for the balance of the Sniping Rifles which has brought up the division to 100 per	JHD.
	14		To ST OMER for the Battalion, which is the number GOC decides to have. New pattern Pesch Plate to drive JHD	
	15		Heard Division is going to take over from 1st Canadian Division & that the 23rd will probably be the most suitable date to change to the new uplines boots. The 3rd Canadian Division are coming to take over this stores. Arranging to leave the 5000 P. Helmets, any of the woven socks & whatever blankets can be exchanged.	JHD.
	16			
	17		Definite instructions that the Division is going for about 10 days into the place of the 3rd Canadian Division. Headquarters to be at FLETRE near BAILLEUL. Most of the outstanding sizes of horseshoes received from Base, namely 8's & 4's	JHD.
	18		To FLETRE to see new store which, altho' small, is a good store. It is intended to only open a small depot here owing to the short period expected. Suspended all stores from the Base. Railhead changes from WIPPENHOEKE to GODEWAERSVELDE from tomorrow 19th.	JHD.

Army Form C. 2118.

WAR DIARY
or
INTELLIGENCE SUMMARY.
(Erase heading not required.)

Instructions regarding War Diaries and Intelligence Summaries are contained in F. S. Regs., Part II. and the Staff Manual respectively. Title pages will be prepared in manuscript.

Place	Date	Hour	Summary of Events and Information	Remarks and references to Appendices
RENINGHELST	March 1916			
	19		To new area to see D.D.O. 3rd Canadian Division to make final arrangements about taking over from him of many Sirus common to both were exchanged. These included D'Helmets, Steel Helmets, satchels etc	f.M.O.
	20		Moved everything to Flêtre about 5 miles west of BAILLEUL. Settled in by midday to quite a food store. Many units had had to dump their winter clothing to save transport, but this was stopped owing to the fact that the necessary arrangements for the reception & return of railway difficulties for all these items has not yet been authorised by the Army. 15th April was the date fixed by the Division.	f.M.O.
FLETRE	21		Heavy demands on tents for many units owing to the fact that the 3rd Canadian renewing any in their possession & insufficient billets could be obtained by some units.	f.M.O.
	22		The R.A. units beginning to come in for stores but no infantry yet	f.M.O.
	23		To new area to see 1st Canadian Div. store with A.D.O.S. A triumph had stores with no accommodation for office therefore for anything else. Map 28 T 25 d.o.o. being reference. About 5 to 6 miles from St Jans Capel which is to be Div. Hqrs. Remove suspension of stores at Base owing to D.O.O. 1st Canadian premises or stores at his dump before I move into his store. Railhead remains at GODEWAERSVELDE until 24th.	f.M.O.

WAR DIARY
or
INTELLIGENCE SUMMARY.

Army Form C. 2118.

Place	Date	Hour	Summary of Events and Information	Remarks and references to Appendices
	March 1916			
FLETRE	24		Went to see another farm which 1st Canadian Machine Gun Co were occupying. As it had now attached to this division this made a good store for A.D. Just about ½ mile outside BAILLEUL on the NIEPPE road - Two good wooden huts up behind the farm & excellent accommodation &c for the men - Only ½ mile from Railhead which is BAILLEUL. J.H.D.	
	25		Tried up to take this farm & also a barn my orderly situated close for receiving the winter clothing. J.H.D.	
	26		Wire from II Army asking for all spade grips to Machine Guns in possession of the Light Mountings to be returned to Base for shipment to England where they are badly needed. Weather beginning to improve, the cars dried. J.H.D.	
	27		After receiving a scheme for the return of winter clothing from the Corps. I have discussed letter published giving exact date of shipping of same for steamers between 1st April & any first fortnight in May after which time it is to be completed. Sent to Paris with the exception of Sheepskins & Boots F.S. & Calais. J.H.D.	
BAILLEUL	29		Moved to new quarters near BAILLEUL - It may be necessary to send lorries to take stores out to some units - Lists of location will not be available until 1st April - J.H.D.	
	30		Several units asking for Jerkins Knives for former Harvey, but have been informed that these was no chance of getting them for some time yet. Hand carts for Stores Guns to not be available until May- J.H.D.	
	31		L/Cpl. Calestri, who has been 5 weeks with the division for instruction in warrant officer's work orders to return to Woolwich which lids at 7.30 tonight. 15 Catapults from 5 Corps for the division - Now needed in this area. J.H.D.	

J.H.D. Kyffin
Capt. D.A.O. 24th Div.

A.D.S.S./Forms/C. 2118

Army Form C. 2118.

24Div
DADOS
Vol 7

WAR DIARY
or
INTELLIGENCE SUMMARY.
(Erase heading not required.)

Instructions regarding War Diaries and Intelligence Summaries are contained in F. S. Regs., Part II. and the Staff Manual respectively. Title pages will be prepared in manuscript.

Place	Date	Hour	Summary of Events and Information	Remarks and references to Appendices
BAILLEUL	April			
	1		Questionable whether a forward dump will not have to be raised for the units around PLOEGSTEERT at present not are coming in but finding it a long way.	
	2		The first day of the return of units private clothing under a scheme to finish on 18 May. Obtained a suitable store where main stores but quite separate to keep these articles. Issues available every four days to carry these items to Paris. Old clothes are divided into 4 groups & as nearly as possible these groups are to be kept to when despatching to the railhead.	JHP JHP
	3		Stores beginning to settle down — Working still by Brigades, each W.O. looking after his own brigade solely with his storeman & clerk. Most satisfactory. Still two for there are 3 separate huts.	JHP
	4		G.O.C. to inspect French Mounting generally to see the new stores	JHP
	5		Winter Clothing in Corps A coming in well, especially jerkins.	JHP
	6		Two extra Lewis guns just issued to Battalions when instructions received that they are all to be drawn in transit to Canadians	JHP
	7		Actual transfer of guns carried out.	JHP
	8		Rumours of II Corps wanting the farm owing to the fact that we were 20 years outside II Corps (V) area.	JHP
	9		Spent considerable time looking on the II Corps area side of BAILLEUL for a suitable store — country very scarce of farm suitable for transport in DRANOUTRE area.	JHP

353. Wt. W4541/7454. 700,000. 8/15. D.D.&L. A.D.S.S./Forms/C.2118.

Army Form C. 2118.

WAR DIARY
or
INTELLIGENCE SUMMARY.
(Erase heading not required)

Place	Date	Hour	Summary of Events and Information	Remarks and references to Appendices
BAILLEUL			April	
	10	-17	Moved into new Store Office at Sq 4.5 Map 28 on the 10th owing to necessity for getting into T Corps area. A good farm & stores the road known a great deal. Quite good in summer but tested in wet weather. Has to reinforce this road with 150 tons of stone in all. Position good for work round BRANOUTRE but found it too far from an advanced dump for this at PLOEGSTEERT. This was situated at B 16 2.4 Map 36 trying on the spot for 3/4 of the winter, being only 500 yards off many-one Brigade H.Q., two stores men took out all stores home to these units. All papers work & control of same done from Sgt 4.5 Stores Office. JHD	
	18		Decided to try magnets for attracting pieces of metal in oats.	
	19		To BOULOGNE to obtain some thing suitable which it was found possible to own to a type the French Govt. was using for same work being obtainable JHD	
	20		Full issue of P.H. helmet up from Base instead of only 5000 JHD	
	21	-30	All gum boots held for a while in spite of W. Clothing Scheme. Steel Helmets coming up with 8000 now in the division. Great question as to whether they should be carried with corps by train to prevent the light Sheum. off. JHD Weather very good & road improving. Advanced Dump working well. JHD	

DAQ
2nd Echelon

Forward please two attached Diary
for May 1916.

A/6/16

J.A.S.Dickinson
Capt D.A.2. 24th Div

WAR DIARY or INTELLIGENCE SUMMARY

Army Form C. 2118.

May 1916

Place	Date	Hour	Summary of Events and Information	Remarks and references to Appendices
BAILLEUL	1		Owing to Gno attack on night of 29th April great demand, at present [amounting] to 70%, of P.H. Helmets being received. These are there are replacing are being withdrawn & sent down to Base for reshipping. 2 Lewis guns up to replace those put out of action on that side.	J.H.D.
	2		A little rain after a weeks very good weather – Last group of Winter clothing beginning to come in. Also, large quantities of blankets received.	J.H.D.
	3		Very large demand on P.H. Helmet – over 14000 exchanges –	J.H.D.
	4		To HAZEBROUCK for 11 Cylinders to be recharged for Gas Alarm stores. Also to MERVILLE for samples of Lewis Machine Gun Carriers, Butchers Knives & a suitable pack for carrying Lewis Gun Magazines – one to carry 8 & one for 6.	J.H.D.
	5		An order that all P.H.G. Helmets were to be recalled & P.H. issued in lieu for time being. The reason said to be that the elastic band inside outside instead of in the helmet. Last group of Winter Clothing coming in well. Many Horse Rugs & Blankets still being received.	J.H.D.
	6		To HAZEBROUCK to get more Gas Alarm Cylinders charged. Jrn to MERVILLE to bring back samples of a Lewis Gun Magazine Carrier, Halo Cook-knife & P.H.G. Helmet. Order to withdraw all P.H.G. Helmet now stopped pending instructions –	J.H.D.
	7		Just over 9000 P.H. Helmets to help bring up Divisional Reserve – 1260 of which are now to be held by the Three Brigades. 3800 Blankets sent off to Base under Winter Clothing arrangements. The Sixth Machine Gun sent down to Base having received up a similar number of new ones to replace those lost destroyed by enemy during last week.	J.H.D.

Army Form C. 2118.

WAR DIARY
or
INTELLIGENCE SUMMARY.
(Erase heading not required.)

Instructions regarding War Diaries and Intelligence Summaries are contained in F.S. Regs., Part II. and the Staff Manual respectively. Title pages will be prepared in manuscript.

Place	Date	Hour	Summary of Events and Information	Remarks and references to Appendices
BAILLEUL	May 8		A No 7 Dial sight receiver for BTob Bryan from Base. The first of these instruments received for months.	
	9		Every officer in the Division has been complied with a steel helmet.	J.J.D.
			To Merville to fix finally on pattern for Cooks knife. Laws for Cooks Knives. Magazine Holster. Demand for 2 more special magnets as per French pattern for extracting metal out of oats. This makes the No. 10 the Divisional Train	J.J.D.
	10		Sixteen Special Type of New French Helmet received for trial.	J.J.D.
	11		To MERVILLE HAZEBROUCK. For Cooks Suits. Thence from centre — Thousands of units Clothing despatched to Paris.	
	12		Over 2000 gum boots received in winter Clothing Scheme. Approximately work carried in sorting tenders. Jam also tarps, jackets, Jams. Another machine gun receiver for N. Staff in lieu of one damaged in recent attack.	J.J.D.
			Divisional Baths are now carrying in clothing repairs, boot & laundry. These articles they have supposed to have themselves. They are being dried separately in the open.	J.J.D.
	13		7000 used nails from Baths to be sent down to Base. 1st Thousand brought in 25th today — Sacks are being used for the packing of these.	J.J.D.

Army Form C. 2118.

WAR DIARY
or
INTELLIGENCE SUMMARY.
(Erase heading not required.)

Instructions regarding War Diaries and Intelligence Summaries are contained in F. S. Regs., Part II. and the Staff Manual respectively. Title pages will be prepared in manuscript.

Place	Date	Hour	Summary of Events and Information	Remarks and references to Appendices
BAILLEUL			May 1916	
	14		Issued a break made take Lewis Magazine back to Cold 8 & another to Cold 6 magazines to 73rd Brigade for that.	
	15		400 Suits for Cooks ready for issue under special authority to the Division.	JHD
	16		Specially made Lewis gun Covers issued to 17 BHQ for trial report	JHD
	17		Winter Clothing nearly all in, & items returned are most satisfactory	JHD
	18		Went actdown until next note received. Capt Baird fm 3rd Division answering for JHD	JHD
	29		The two extra Lewis Machine guns per battalion together with 15 magazines receives up to issued.	JHD
	30		An extra 170 magazines up towards full complement for each gun of above being approximately 1/3 of that required for the division.	JHD
	31		11000 Grease Boots for knees received, sent down to the Base, leaving only 800 odd pairs in the division for summer months	JHD

J.H.D.Steppard
Capt DSO. 24th Divn

24 June 1916

DADOS

WAR DIARY
or
INTELLIGENCE SUMMARY.

Army Form C. 2118.

9.10

Place	Date	Hour	Summary of Events and Information	Remarks and references to Appendices
BAILLEUL	June 1916		A.D.O. 24th Division	
	1		The second S.D.? chit received from the Base - The question of whether the final blanket is to be withdrawn from the new in shape - 5308 ahead in awaits decn	
	2		Instructions received that Sniping School (Army) are now going to repair & keep up a port to meet additional requirements.	
	3		Lt. J.H. Morris arrived for duty with S.D.O.	
	4		16 Battle Sights received for 73 M.Gun Coy.	
	5		Jo Menin to get after Special Carts for Lewis Guns made for 17th Brigade fitted	
	6		Change in the weather, considerable quantity of rain.	
	7		A small quantity of the new Lewis Gun carts sent up for the Base reserve - his Corn does not go out to Laurel at all turn not G. out the fixing a magazine to fitter. Otherwise seems a most serviceable item.	
	8 to 15		To railhead to see about the dispatch of unserviceable clothing - Paris now receives any sundry clothing or service dress for repair even if not disinfected provided it is properly laundered & sacked - A good deal been received from 9th Bath Durham unserviceable clothing which cannot be repaired have only the fit for rags and are sent to Calais for shipment home to Ming	
	16.		Up evening about 9.30pm Enemy's 2nd Lt flare - 5800 Helmets had to be sent up to them 70 in the middle of the right - 72nd Brigade got the worst part of the Cloud.	
	17 to		Weather fair - Everything much as usual. N. Eglise arranged dumps broken somewhat Stores coming up from Calais & quickly - 18 Bn etc wired for H.Q. 4.30pm dn Cavn.	
	25.		A.D.O. come round to inspect stores	
	26.			
	27/6		A lot of time fractured has to be put on new road to & round the store being laid off whilst new rail was being put over the old road in 2 places.	
	30		From O/c Road at BAILLEUL forward to BAILLEUL Station on Baingem railroad. J.H. Flitcroft Capt. S.O. 24 Div	

WAR DIARY
or
INTELLIGENCE SUMMARY.
(Erase heading not required.)

Army Form C. 2118.

Place	Date	Hour	Summary of Events and Information	Remarks and references to Appendices
BAILLEUL			July 1916	
	1		All winter clothing now sent to Base including 2nd blanket with the exception of 25% allowed to be retained for summer months.	ftd.
	2		Instructions to demand the 7th & 8th Lewis Gun per Battalion received.	
	3		Owing to a new railway cutting road to store in two places me a level crossing the other four feet above the roadlevel considerable distance has been added to the journey to railhead tabs for units drawing stores. However this is only last Temp – Bivouac moving a little further North but still a question whether it will not be best to stay in same place for a time.	ftd.
			Beginning to get a slot cut road on to Dranoutre road a distance of only 200 yards but this was never used for more than one month for the purpose of vehicles such year – Manuls due to high explosion shells keeping most light fair lorries with Brig around to Bury Kenne: Eglise abraneus store for 17/173rd Brigade working very well under Acting W.O. Rebin.	ftd.
	4		Nothing of any importance; divisions requiring a great many special stores at very short notice making it necessary to spend a lot of time in local purchase gun stores such as Bail French Dinoters etc still seem impossible to reach.	ftd.
	5 6 7 8		L/Moreus attached to the Division again. Weather fair – Divisional Headquarters moved to LOCRE but it was not necessary to move the store –	ftd.

Army Form C. 2118.

WAR DIARY
or
INTELLIGENCE SUMMARY.

(Erase heading not required.)

S.D.O. 24th Division

Instructions regarding War Diaries and Intelligence Summaries are contained in F.S. Regs., Part II. and the Staff Manual respectively. Title pages will be prepared in manuscript.

Place	Date	Hour	Summary of Events and Information	Remarks and references to Appendices
BAILLEUL	July 1916			
	9.7.16		Last night about midnight orders were received to obtain 300 Australian type felt hats & to deliver them to three different units in the division before daybreak. Those orders came thro' 9 brough having 3 trucks from 9th Corps under whom the Australian Division now come. Took the car to BAILLY SUR LA LYS where the 4th Australian Division had Rec'd dumps obtained the hats returning afterwards delivering them according to a scheme allotment at ENGLISH FARM & TRANOUTRE by the 24th Division & the hats went to be worn to try the Anzac front had to be taken over by the 24th Division & the hats went to be worn to try & keep the enemy in ignorance of the Change. Sufficient P.H.G. Helmets were today required to equip the whole division with one per officer & man. Orders have been issued for the return of our P.H. 50's replaces. JMD Divisional HeadQuarters moved back to BAILLEUL after being in LOCRE for 5 days. JMD	
	10.7.16		Railhead changed to Steenwerk, instructions to be a temporary change only. Jan less useful than BAILLEUL as further away by 3 miles over bad roads.	
	11.7.16		To LOCRE taking Sickle millears etc. for O.C. "Command Defences" - then to IX Corps Troops for periscopes (100g) which were left with Div. HeadQuarters on way back - J.M.D.	
	12.7.16		Road from S3d63 thro' 29 to 93e made passable for light traffic. This road has been of no use for a very long period but by draining, tracks, dam, etc. has now become quite serviceable. The work was carried out by the Pioneer Regiments & Ammunition Park during their spare time.	
	13.7.16			

WAR DIARY / INTELLIGENCE SUMMARY

Army Form C. 2118.

D.A.D.O.S. 24th Division

Place	Date	Hour	Summary of Events and Information	Remarks and references to Appendices
BAILLEUL	July (continued) 1916			
	14.7.16		To HAZEBROUCK for local purchases, white tape & urgently required. Considerable difficulty in obtaining same owing to the date being a fête day. Town shops shut + however several of our large Lorries (A.T.S.) were sent off & very soon arrived back with our private hire sent up some supplies. Called also at H.M. Workshops to have several Strength Cylinders refilled.	JHD
	15.7.16		To advanced Dump at Meavis & also down to R.O.D. STEENWERCK to arrange for transport of 900 blankets to the Base.	JHD
	16.7.16		Lt MOWELLS to MONT NOIR 9th Corps H.Q. to take over Stores from Camp Commandant – 9th Corps going South. 124th Div. handed over back to V Corps – Railhead for forward BAILLEUL as before.	JHD
	17.7.16		Lt MOWELLS to MONT NOIR with Fatigue Party to bring tentage to Ord. by 9th Corps to 24th Div. Ordnance Dump – F.C.M. in action Sub Contractor Peachy ref 17.7.18. Visited Advanced Dump at NEUVE EGLISE – Car broken down. Sent into Supply Column for repair. Remaining tentage brought from MONT NOIR. Visited Salvage Dump.	JHD
	18.7.16 to 19.7.16		Sudden orders received to move out to Italy – 20th Division to take over from us. This was next cancelled + finally we moved to ST JANS CAPPEL on 23rd. Made a stop on a big green patch near the roadside with a letter tent + marquee. Evacuated to the Base all hands over to incoming division as many Stores as would not be required to keep a little Reserve of Everything in the Lorry on hearing we were going South.	JHD
	23.7.16		Formulated Evidence in Action Sub Contractor Peachy.	
	24.7.16		Settled down at ST JANS CAPPEL – Made arrangements with A.D.R.T. HAZEBROUCK to take the whole R.A. Helmet reserve by train. These were sent to CAESTRE the afternoon + loaders together with the Armourers kit into 3 wagons.	JHD
	25.7.16		Section Lorry started at 10 a.m. for PICQUIGNY via St Pol. Div. finally had to entrain at CAVILLON about 2 miles nearer Abbeville where a small station was	

WAR DIARY
INTELLIGENCE SUMMARY

Army Form C. 2118.

Place	Date	Hour	Summary of Events and Information	Remarks and references to Appendices
	July (continued) 1916		D.D.O. 24th Division	
	to 26.7.16		Started & a certain amount of stores tried.	
	27.7.16		To ABBEVILLE HQ. IGC (ORDNANCE) for some special vans to be made which Sergeant wanted also for some clothing from depot there. The vans were sent down army to take long time stores was taken to arrive from Army Base Ordnance to supply the division has been transferred from CALAIS. JHD	
	28) /16 to 30.7.16		Acting for (indister Peachy returned to Base having been ordered to visits of Corporal of a clerk received in his place. He left a vacancy for the Sergeants clerk & act as H.O. & another Brigade clerk to act as Sergeant Clerk on Divisional Troops JHD work - Attached to 9th Corps.	
	31.7.16		Moved up to CORBIE having to carry all the smoke Helmet reserve. Now transferred to 13th Corps - 13th Corps took a minor role in the troop. JHD	

J.H.D. Shepherd
Capt. D.O. 24th Div.

A.A. & Q.M.G.
24th Div

24(c)/371

Subject:- War Diary

With reference to your a/47/88/8 dated 26/8/16 the copies of June & July War Diaries have been sent to D.A.S. 3rd Echelon to-day & August is forwarded herewith -

J.H.S. Sheppard
Capt D.A.A.G. 24th Div

2/9/16

Army Form C. 2118.

WAR DIARY
or
INTELLIGENCE SUMMARY.
(Erase heading not required.)

Davis

DSO 2nd Division

Vol II

Place	Date	Hour	Summary of Events and Information	Remarks and references to Appendices
CORBIE	1.8.16 to 3.8.16		Division settling round CORBIE & DAOURS as a short rest on the way up to the line. Took a somewhat indifferent old barn in the town as a store, but ere much knew they would soon be moving again & few hours were made. 20 French standards brought in by AAH Vickers workshops. This is a most useful article which we carry around with us — many cases found. Salvage dumps.	
MORLANCOURT	3.8.16		Stopped one night here before going up to filiform tree as a store. This is put on open piece of ground just on the BRAY-ALBERT road about midway but nearer BRAY.	
FILIFORM TREE	4.8.16 to 10.8.16		Put up a marquee tent here for a dump fire. Took over from HQ 30th Division — got the telephone fixed up at once which makes a great deal of difference. Its lately evacuated whilst 2nd Division in reserve. Half the Lewis standards at last received. Railhead DERNACOURT or EDGEHILL as it has recently been termed. 40 minutes run for the lorries.	
	11.8.16		No washing arrangements in this corps at all at present.	
	12.8.16		Weather has been terribly hot but today slight change. Some rain. Stores beginning to get (Scottish?) finish drawing regularly.	
	13.8.16		A small viewer of one of the most important stores completed. A tent repaired. Ordnance is opened at the CITADEL where Staff Captain RA is also near Div HQ. This was done with a view to hastening the departure of things with artillery — in practice there was of little use as we WO was rather not to the Division if not - it is not of the day. Some sent by petrol. Offer were bring & to Y telephone has broken down. full system adopted by the corps for running out stores in demanding shops & tools for RE. Report them to the ADOS its primarily task. Orders were given to keep in readiness 9 days reserve ration & Camp transport. R Regt - Slow spring were notified that this three legions being put into order from them. There will now be the part of 9 Eng move myself. Next day we changed Capo.	
	14.8.16		Jo Railhead AMIENS by an urgent demand of the 9th British material for aeroplane signalling from Infantry. From Divns. The admin Brig D by 14th Corps visited of 13th	
	15.8.16 16.8.16		Jo AMIENS by Lalouce of Division Pacific cars being hired. CRA - for aeroplane - 16 days to Brigade itself for No 14 Rehearse up from the same place as being the farm. Corse Canvas Bed. two hundred Flathy my orderlies towards 2 tin authorized for Camps & stretcher Bearers.	
	20.8.16		Both 2.5 D.R. van car Artillery Lime fired Filtration dull to absence of spares - running out - more expected. Got a few 20 heavy & Oval from A & H Lts Workshops. ADSS/Forms C. 2118 Apices 3/15. D.D.&L. Aires 3, seen 2/per. Stuff 2000/2nd. ADoS. Promise some from his Corps. Transport To Calibre to See - 177 Sprins arrived from France which should finally kit up the front 2 MTs but more received to date.	

WAR DIARY
INTELLIGENCE SUMMARY.

ADS 24th Div

Army Form C. 2118.

Place	Date	Hour	Summary of Events and Information	Remarks and references to Appendices
	21.8.16		August 1916 Continued – Division in action. Demand for 7 Lewis & 2 Vickers Guns & also 2 Light Trench Mortars.	JHD
	22.8.16		Notification received that 2nd Div Artillery no longer to be attached to 24th for Ordnance services. They have been attached for a week, leaving a Sergt Clerk & one storeman. Orders that 2nd Division are taken over from 24th that Corps back to Divisional – Not necessary to move stores at present as 24th have plenty to run next door. All unit gun demands yesterday have been received.	JHD
	23.8.16		To Boves to arrange about a warm contract – no tailors in this area. Supplying soap, Kaki pants Shirts, Socks – Worked at one Army Ordnance & authorising half penny respirators.	JHD
	24.8.16		Division moves out to FORKED TREE. 72 Punjab very badly off for clothing. Steel hats impossible to get from base. Getting small quantities from Railheads & Corps Transport. Now under 4th Corps.	JHD
	25.8.16		Orders received to move – Division back to BUIRE. Saw an Ordnance District E7 C.82 Map 62. Just a field – put up Stores tents & Marquee.	JHD
	26.8.16		Division settling down in bivouacs – Weather fair – Lorry outing action broken & spring – Now under 15th Corps. Left Artillery to 5th Division. Who took over from 24th Div. A warrant Officer was left to 5th Div for the purpose.	JHD
	27.8.16		All losses in magazines now up – Division again complete. Not nearly so many faulty springs after armourers had done the same before issue – 1.5% approx nebs being defective. Very bad weather resembling April in every respect. Constant showers.	JHD
	28.8.16		Running out tin spouts & 18 pr Cannulus Fuses. Sent direct to XV Corps workshops in XV Corps where our guns are & the sent when out of action. To Amiens for special Brass wood for brush polo.	JHD
	29.8.16		Base wire 1400 now still Methodos on rail. Reinforcements continue to arrive without them. Hear Division is taken over from 33rd / 14 Divs. To 33rd Ordnance Star at E. Ilcentral & heamzani.	JHD
	30.8.16		Division moving up to the line – 33rd & 14th Div Artillery transferred to 24th for Ordnance Services.	JHD
	31.8.16		Railhead changes to ALBERT.	JHD

J.H.H. Deshris
Capt. DOO 24th Div

A/4/88/8

D.A.D.O.S.

A Report has been received from A/Q 3rd Echelon, Base to the effect that your War Diary for the months of June & July last have not yet been received.

Will you please expedite & report dispatch hereon

G Mattam
Capt
by Major.
D.A.A. & Q.M.G. 74th Division

26/8

WAR DIARY / INTELLIGENCE SUMMARY

Army Form C. 2118.

500.24 — Division

Vol 12

Place	Date	Hour	Summary of Events and Information	Remarks and references to Appendices
ALBERT Sm/62D Epernay	1.9.16		September 1916. Took over the stores left by 33rd Div Ordnance & put up Sign "Ordnance tent". 700 steel hats received from Base. 1937 Machine Gun Corps lot 5 complete leather Jerkins. Weather fine — lorries able to move in the ground round stores which is only stubble field. When many lorries are unloaded the PH Helmet become apparent & difficult (as division records of 20000) it would appear to be much more practical for the Ordnance Corps troops to hold these. To arrange for Divisional Badges & some female carriers urgently required by 73rd Brigade.	JHD
	2.9.16		700 Steel Helmets received this morning, the Division and now complete. Reinforcements still arrive without helmets. 14th Div Artillery Stores arrives together with a clerk. — Both the 33rd & Div Artillery have kept in a separate tent to run quite independently, except their demands & invoices which are all checked in this office.	JHD
	4.9.16		Sending a load of washing to BOVES but in addition to 8 bags required for same they handed all requirements which has to be done by other people. Total kinds being 14 great taken into account the time taken by the Indian before washing. 500 more Steel Helmets advised from Havre.	JHD
	5.9.16		Items Division coming out for rest apparently going by list track near ABBEVILLE	JHD
	6.9.16		To PONT REMY as Hut was to be at H.Q., found a good site for office etc., 5000 PH Helmets but on rail for new men together with trench articles, 5 handkerchiefs — surprised to see if all stores from the lorries sent on to new area which is known to be AILLY HAUT CLOCHER Bacon & Fritso formation of 33rd & 14th Div Artillery & 7th & 55th Division respectively —	JHD
	7.9.16		to ALBERT to bring back Railhead VIGNACOURT. Setting down the depot begins camping	JHD
AILLY LE HUTCLOUIS	6.9.16 / 8.9.16		Any wet weather makes work difficult... Saw ADS IX Corps	

Army Form C. 2118.

WAR DIARY
or
INTELLIGENCE SUMMARY.
(Erase heading not required.)

Instructions regarding War Diaries and Intelligence Summaries are contained in F. S. Regs., Part II. and the Staff Manual respectively. Title pages will be prepared in manuscript.

Place	Date	Hour	Summary of Events and Information	Remarks and references to Appendices
			September 1916	
AILLY LE HAUT CLOCHER	19.9.16		Orders to move into First Army area, also that Supply Corrie will not accompany Divisions to new army area. Consequently all stores including the Lewis Guns, Lewis Guns to be taken down & put on railroad. Train did not leave until 3.30 pm owing to a detraining station at midnight. Accordingly difficulty in obtaining anything for meals & at the time of night.	App. 24th Division [JHD]
BRUAY	20.9.16		Attachments have an offices tete-en-pictures by 30.4.16	[JHD]
	21.9.16		Head Quarters was probably part of it when the 9th Division —	[JHD]
	22.9.16		Went to see new Site at ESTREE-COUCHIE but found it would be a very poor one for the winter.	[JHD]
	23.9.16		Removal Suspensions & stores. Saw ADS. Now kept at old site in SHQ village at CAMBLAIN L'ABBE which is a much nicer & cleaner place.	[JMD]
ESTRE to CAUCHIE	24.9.16 to 30.9.16		Found it impossible but the stores remained so last here me in ESTRE-CAUCHIE about 2 miles out. He at Bruan has been very tape as it was not such a bad store - Moved into the building on the 27th. Began to get settled in by the end of month. Railroad was a long way off being at BRUAY stn. Winter Clothing being due on 15th of next month. All bulk demands have been prepared so a but have off at the earliest moment.	[JHD]

J.H.D. Stannard
Captain DADOS 24 Div.

D.A.G
3rd Echelon

Herewith War Diaries
for October & November

J.H.S Sheppard
Capt
DADOS 2/4 Div?

26/12/16.

WAR DIARY
or
INTELLIGENCE SUMMARY.
(Erase heading not required.)

Place	Date	Hour	Summary of Events and Information	Remarks and references to Appendices
ESTRÉE CAUCHY	1.X.16		October 1916	
	2.X.16			
	3.X.16			
	4.X.16			
	5.X.16 to 15.X.16			
	16.X.16 to 22.X.16			
	23.X.16			
	24.X.16 to 31.X.16			

WAR DIARY or INTELLIGENCE SUMMARY

Army Form C. 2118.

A.D.O. 24th Division

Place	Date	Hour	Summary of Events and Information	Remarks and references to Appendices
BRACQUEMONT	1.XI.16		Moved into new Store taken over from 40th Division. At present Store with armourers Shop complete. The officers' men's accommodation in a separate building & not suitable probably to that Store the Divisional Ordnance has ever had. Took over the 40th Div Artillery Kept 24 Fd behind in old area. New ammn store not to them as they were not far off & taught to the comm anyhow. This is extraordinary when permission is not kept to books straight. The Div/Sion now comes into 1st Corps area.	JHD
	2.XI.16 to 11.XI.16		On leave	
	12.XI.16		Started Divisional Boot Shop having in all with 4 pts some the Infantry Bn who have their own bootmakers. However where they cannot cope with the work they can send boots in for repair in these necessary cases. The Div Boot Shop is undoubtedly a good idea provided the Division remains for some considerable period in one place & there is sufficient accommodation which is the case here. Also the necessary branch requires to send boots down to the Base for repair being beyond the means of the Armourers Shop. Considerably keeping in the armourers in Division. Gave 3 (i.e. one to each Brigade) starting to get all the Divn men a month funds to New Xmas so much less work to do in each the small ordnance equipment which must kept up to now. & by men then but don't can be sure. The new target & identity discs are now coming up there stamped for (ind) rest of the division by men under the supervision of an armourer for (ind)	JHD

Army Form C. 2118.

WAR DIARY
or
INTELLIGENCE SUMMARY.
(Erase heading not required.)

Instructions regarding War Diaries and Intelligence Summaries are contained in F. S. Regs., Part II. and the Staff Manual respectively. Title pages will be prepared in manuscript.

Place	Date	Hour	Summary of Events and Information	Remarks and references to Appendices
B.H.Q. 74th Division	November (contd) 1916			
	21.XI.16 to 26.XI.16		All units are now complete with the new Box Respirator. The 10% reserve is kept in the Stores of these items. Considerable trouble is being found with the main of Stewart Clippers this year. Chains for same are badly made & always breaking. Pliers seem to be no means of getting these replaced. Electric Torch refills have been impossible to get lately which has caused an immense amount of inconvenience to many units. A firm last repairing shop has been started but up to the present time has not been of much work for these men.	JHO
	27.XI.16		To railhead in morning & out on Divis practice during afternoon	JHO
	28.XI.16		Visited QM.S. Stores of 72nd Brigade - Most of these are well kept & such however not found.	JHO
	29.XI.16 to 30.XI.16		A.O.D. visited stores also store of the Division. Weather setting in bad too. Question of Right for Ammunition Dump keeping quite a necessary worth. Put in for 3 Cyclists to assist. The WO. Great difficulty in getting sufficient wagons for the vehicles of the Division. Base cannot supply.	JHO

J.H.O'Neill
Capt. DADOS 74 Division

Army Form C. 2118.

WAR DIARY
or
INTELLIGENCE SUMMARY.
(Erase heading not required.)

Instructions regarding War Diaries and Intelligence Summaries are contained in F. S. Regs., Part II. and the Staff Manual respectively. Title pages will be prepared in manuscript.

Place	Date	Hour	Summary of Events and Information	Remarks and references to Appendices
BRACQUEMONT	1.12.16		Saw A.D.O.S. re horse transport for the Division generally. Great difficulty in obtaining same from Base. All wheels have a tremendous amount of punishment, generally the position in this respect is very bad.	
	2.12.16		A table was drawn up to get all the materials known to the division into Shops in turn for several small alterations including the strengthening of the brakes talkatively to prevent JMD light Mobile	
	3.12.16 to 13.2.16		A tremendous number of orders passing thro Armourer's Shop. A great effort is being made to take in all the machines known to shew to require necessary to prevent the great neglect of same by units. There is great difficulty in obtaining sufficient armourers for the division. JMD	
	14 13.12.16		Baths driven very heavily from hour to hour & consequently enormous quantity of clothing from this department by Laundry. The present system is v. inadequate required for such a big question involving as it does the use or sum of thousands of pounds of clothing. It seems a Corps only should run the baths since they can run a man or less permanent staff than not have to be ready so mobile as a Division. At present there is really nothing in which O.O.'s can check or Base terms for Laundries demands. Since the Dryer facilities are always apparent in each area the stock must also fluctuate. Hence no fixed form in which to check can be obtained. This should obviously be under a capable Officer. Also the question of khaki serial itself should be in possession of this Officer. Authorised clothing of Remounts into the Baths wants decision. JMD	

8353 Wt. W3544/1454 700,000 5/15 D.D. & L. A.D.S.S./Forms/C. 2118.

WAR DIARY
INTELLIGENCE SUMMARY

Army Form C. 2118.

Place	Date	Hour	Summary of Events and Information	Remarks and references to Appendices
	December 1916 (contd)		W.A.D.D. 9th Division	
	26-31st		The question of load of troops & Bn. tps. also requires more thought. Large quantities are sent out two possible check can be made own to the tremendous fluctuation circumstances — Washing out done by the women near the Laundry seems a very unsanitary practice. Since it has a tendency of spoiling the uniform & if the uniforms in any size or quantity needs to each woman then employer, it is impossible to Remonstrate due to the Ministry of Munitions being concerned. Weather rather colder. Capresico now has with A.D.O.S. Boot Shop doing extraordinary good work — an average of 80 pairs being repaired daily by 8 men. The Gum Boot Store has now been turned into a shop for repairs. Same where 3 men have been until employed — Attendance no shortage of Electric Light refills to torches. JND	JND JND JH Shepherd Capt RAMC

WAR DIARY
INTELLIGENCE SUMMARY

Vol 16
Army Form C. 2118.

Dated 24th January

Place	Date	Hour	Summary of Events and Information	Remarks and references to Appendices
BRAQUEMONT	1.1.17 to 24.1.17		Visited Railhead front into Mervin & 18m. Heavy workshops for rifle mechanism for Mervin motors. The supply of these items is not much altered, yet the workshop has been frightfully hot whenever the account. The turntable mould lies with the steel hat the bars can be turned on that, which is driven into the cartridge chamber in order to take the special shape ammunition for this work. Black powder is used being hot in the cartridge with a view to diminishing the recoil of breaking too many mechanisms. In this way, that a number of ordinary S.A.A. cases have been filled in improvised Armourers shop with black powder treated to meet the urgent requirements & so far after rifle mechanisms without the least return is sent. This saves the considerable amount of time taken by H. Mobile Shop MERVILLE to produce these items — the 'S' base of Capstan lathes put to the work.	
	20.1.17		Weather extremely cold. Severe frost & very heavy snow. Local purchase BETHUNE & watch field Cashier calling at H.M. Workshop to pay Persian Mechanics. 8 Major Keith in charge.	
	24.1.17 to 31.1.17		Good work done in Divisional Armourers Shop with 10 Armourers including Asstn. S. Major Keith in charge. AM cycles Mrs put the Division having had nearly 350 pairs of boots are put in future to pass thro' the H.Q. Armourers Shop once a month to prevent any wear at Som... The work done in Divisional Boot Shop is of great value not only by the amount of repair work, every hole ime being stitched by the armourer. The boots now being supplied from Base are requiring a tremendous amount of stitching really, require a machine for closing the work. The old clothing returned now is stained beyond redress against further wear. Considerable trouble been experienced with the ignition affairs of French Motors (Peugeot.) The dept of these H. Q. P. S. at Armantieres being of the too. Men a month there are commonly for repair actually been done by Indian & full Mechanics are temporary magneto. Motors at all other workshops for H. Q. P. S. at District.	

J. H. Stewart, Capt R.A.O.D., Cdt. 2nd Division.

Army Form C. 2118.

WAR DIARY
or
INTELLIGENCE SUMMARY.
(Erase heading not required.)

9/5/17 D.A.D.O. 9th Division

Place	Date	Hour	Summary of Events and Information	Remarks and references to Appendices
BRACQUEMONT	1·2·17 to 10·2·17		February 1917 On leave. Capt WINCH C t. Divisional Ordnance Officer doing duty for me	
	11·2·17 & 12·2·17		Weather very severe much snow & exceptionally hard frost. Division going back to rest round the LABEUVRIE area. An store premise been cut down despatched to Base. Went over to see the proposed store at LABEUVRIÉ, an old tile factory. a most suitable place but just doubtful if the owner would hand over own to requirin to recommence making tiles.	
LABEUVRIE	13·2·17		Moved into TILE FACTORY at LABEUVRIÉ. Quite a suitable store & offices after getting Electric light fitted. Considerable difficulty experienced with the roads due to have precautions. Railhead at LILLERS & no lorries allowed from Store to main road. Special authority had to be obtained from the Army on several occasions. Over the Divisional Train had to bring the Stores from the Main road to the Ordnance Store. Loads were brought from railhead to the point by lorries. The state of the roads getting very bad indeed too many cars they had to be closed. J.M.D.	
	20·2·17			

Army Form C. 2118.

WAR DIARY
or
INTELLIGENCE SUMMARY.
(Erase heading not required).

Instructions regarding War Diaries and Intelligence Summaries are contained in F. S. Regs., Part II. and the Staff Manual respectively. Title pages will be prepared in manuscript.

Place	Date	Hour	Summary of Events and Information	Remarks and references to Appendices
LABEUVRIE	21.2.17		February 1917 (continued) A.D.O.S. 94th Division	
	22.2.17 to 28.2.17		To Railhead - Visited by A.D.O.S in afternoon. A small issue of Special Steel Helmets fitted with what is called a Vizor was made. The Vizor is a net of chains hung on the eyes behind the nose when properly fixed is a taut manner, those intended to keep the eyes free from a blow from soda or bits of stone thrown about from a bursting shell - However they were found to be of little use there not favourably reported on. The limit etc in use the helmet was of a much more superior description any previously seen. Units drawing a good many stores to a partial refit. H.Q. of the Division in same billet. Weather still very severe. Since post supply has now been made of Limbered F.S. Wagons for carrying Lewis Machine Guns and the Lewis Hand Cart same type Battalion have been despatched to the Base.	

J.H.D. Stevens –
Capt. D.A.D.O.S. 24th Division

WAR DIARY
or
INTELLIGENCE SUMMARY
(Erase heading not required.)

Army Form C. 2118.

A.D.O.S. 24th. Division

Place	Date	Hour	Summary of Events and Information	Remarks and references to Appendices
LABEUVRIE	1.3.17 to 4.3.17	March 1917	Division to move at any time now back to the line to a little South of its last position in the Loos Salient. ST.H.Q. to go to BARLIN - Could not set the store at BRACQUEMONT just vacated before being without accn owing to 6th Division H.Q. being close by them consequently their I.O.S.'s was not able to move out. Hence in spite of 6th. Division being North of 24th. Div. the only place for its Ordnance was NOEUX LES MINES with railhead at that station.	/H.S./
NOEUX LES MINES	5.3.17 to 20.3.17		Moved to NOEUX LES MINES, took all stores & personal kit over - Settled into a moderate office & rather scattered store places there - Difficulty to get an Armourers Shop there close at hand, but finally got quite a good one which altho' small answered the purpose. Weather still very severe - Alternating snow & sleet - very cold. Stores coming up to new railhead quite satisfactorily, trains starting to come in quite well. Still in S.P. Caps. Acting A.D.O.S. visited store topics. Great shortage of electric refills for ordinary S.P. Torch. Many has to be obtained by L. Purchase. This entails one of a small wood connecting piece as the only available refills given are equal voltage but of Sgt. pattern is much shorter. Large demands on Gum boots due to wastage in the line. 3 men kept in repair of these boots in Gum Boot Shop which certainly helps out the position.	/H.S./ /H.S./

WAR DIARY
or
INTELLIGENCE SUMMARY.

(Erase heading not required.)

Army Form C. 2118.

Place	Date	Hour	Summary of Events and Information	Remarks and references to Appendices
			March 1917 (continued) BASES 47th Division	
NOEUX LES MINES	21.3.17 to 31.3.17		Great trouble to keep up supply of Breech Mechanisms. Doing what can be done in Armourers Shop to repair any possible & help out Heavy Mobile Shops. However most of the repairs are of the nature of latte work. Broken B.M.s + ordinary .303 cases filled with black powder issued in emergencies to some effect.	
			Considerable inconvenience at Ruitz through Staff due to the rapidly shelling of the former. The strays which flew uncomfortably near the office. On three occasions the women had to stopped (only in afternoon there of no practical consequence) the staff sent out into the fields leaving the stores padlocked. This trouble got worse & worse as time went on.	
			Head Division H.Q. were going shortly up to PETIT SAINS however there was little point in moving the stores over this small distance. Great shortage of the leather from the Base. Had to buy considerable quantities to keep Divisional + Battallion Boot Shop supplied. Supplies of spares/kip was v. high but it was found latter seemed at time advantageous taking into account the price of a new boot (1£ approx.), that men lying idle, extra transport to Base, poorer type of boot coming up from Base at the time acquiring sudden strain; After a weeks wear. However it was afterwards found not to be advantageous - Hob nails v. difficult to obtain from Base. Quantities of French H. nail purchased at a reasonable price. These unfortunately give since little to the boot. It was found that its leather from bottoms of boots (old) could be utilised for so him to a considerable degree which in dry weather would become quite a useful saving. Two entrenching mallets off the old leather being the disadvantage. A boot machine for stitching also employed to great advantage. SMS.	

Army Form C. 2118.

Vol 19

WAR DIARY
or
INTELLIGENCE SUMMARY.
(Erase heading not required.)

A.D.M.S. 24th Division

Place	Date	Hour	Summary of Events and Information	Remarks and references to Appendices
NOEUX LES MINES	1.4.17 to 21.4.17		April 1917	
			Issues proceeding as usual. Rations being drawn a certain amount each day & the Divis by A.D.S. A good many Special Stores such as pack saddles, Special Rations sacks etc being used the Division.	
			Owing to great shortage on return of stores time to time — Has a S.R.O. pillars & the private steps taken to ensure 15 percentage returned. Weather lately has been extremely bad — Alternate sun & rain.	
			LT SHERRIFF rejoined its division for his new instruction having been several divisions to DADOS letter.	
			A great deal of local purchase has had to be resorted to lately. Considerable difficulty kept from Base Soap, Soda, starch, torch refills, leather hob nail + nose bags —	
			Head Qr division is to move back into rest area & stations are — Division HQ the NORRENT FONTES altin town & further one at FONTES Head Qrs: —	
FONTES	22.4.17		Moved everything to FONTES. Division beginning to need enormous stores of Clothing boots equipment & necessaries. They have had a bad time at	

Army Form C. 2118.

WAR DIARY
or
INTELLIGENCE SUMMARY.

(Erase heading not required.)

Instructions regarding War Diaries and Intelligence Summaries are contained in F. S. Regs., Part II. and the Staff Manual respectively. Title pages will be prepared in manuscript.

Place	Date	Hour	Summary of Events and Information	Remarks and references to Appendices
			ADMS 24th Division	
FONTES	22.4.17 to 30.4.17 (contd)		April 1917 (continued) LIEVIN & require a bn. reft. The distances make it difficult. Raillies at Liévin. One Brigade (72 IB) to BOMY & which place 3.14.0 has now moved. One Brigade in BETHUNE area. The 73rd round HOUCHIN. Water. Clothing dumps have been fixed at HOUCHIN & RECLINGHEM. Now in II Corps. A.D.O. has been on several times. Everything going on with twenties fine that. JHDS	

J.H.D.Sheppas.
Capt SANDS 24th Division

WAR DIARY or INTELLIGENCE SUMMARY

Army Form C. 2118.

LANES. 24th Division

Place	Date	Hour	Summary of Events and Information	Remarks and references to Appendices
FONTES	1.5.17 to 15.5.17		Division still very scattered – 72nd & Divisional Troops together with Gunners at a distance of 15 miles from Ordnance Store Traffic. Their lorries being sent out from here to two refilling points, each of three A.S.C. or Sergeant Clerks has to be sent with a Convoy of lorries daily – COYECQUE & Pt SENLIS (MAP 5A HAZEBROUCK) being the two R.P's respectively, but these places were changed a little from day to day as occasion for a new Entente dump became necessary. The 17th I.B. were being supplied by Column which dumped at BETHUNE & 73rd I.B. at HOUCHIN each taking their W. Office Rationman. Railhead at LILLERS to the Ammun. of Gunners to the Enemy is very great, hints from their winds to M.S.W.O.'s at R. Points takes their back any item required to be repaired in Armourer Shop its together with old Clothing. This last item often amounting to a full lorry load from each Brigade. The whole division has been refitting & drawing very large numbers of all Service Dress & Boots. This was due to the long time it has just recently had at LIÉVIN. Divisional HQ moves in from BOMY back to NORRENT FONTES for a few days before going into II Army Area on 12th May. At Present it is at WINNEZEELE. 64 Lewis Guns were issued to take the Hotch Kiss for carrying out making to Division Snipers except for half K. 17-18.	

WAR DIARY
INTELLIGENCE SUMMARY.

BASED 24th Division

Place	Date	Hour	Summary of Events and Information	Remarks and references to Appendices
POPERINGE G.14.b.Central (Map 28)	16.5.17 to 22.5.17		May 1917 (Continued) Settling down in new store which has been partly made by 15th Corps – Heavy work. State where All units coming in with the exception of DAC. 106 Brigade & 174 Coy Divisional Train. Stores being run out to these units refilling points near Cassel. Weather v. fine. Sent from ADS– also BASED II Army who came to so into (spares for Vickers & Lewis Guns Spares required the stocked by II Army from Park which is just about to open. 250 Yukon packs issued to the Division – these seem the a most useful article 300 Hammocks (of a naval design) also being issued. A.D.O. of the Corps Contests an Stalter's tents which are being issued to permitse an Approbation being made from H.Q Division.	J.H.D.
	23.5.17		To HAZEBROUCK re special water carrying packs for Pesos this which II Army R.E. workshops are supplying.	J.H.D.
	24.5.17		Railhead at WIPPENHOEK. Consolidated indent for anti-dimin. parts for supplies on Box Respirators passed to Peace – Winter Clothing has been quite withdrawn only a very few items still with units being returned – A very good return for the whole Division. Was all sent into two selected unit dump & top representatives there & taken to LILLERS + BETHUNE railheads respectively by A.O.F Lorries.	J.H.D.

Army Form C. 2118.

WAR DIARY
or
INTELLIGENCE SUMMARY.
(Erase heading not required.)

Army Troops 24th Div Slow

Place	Date	Hour	Summary of Events and Information	Remarks and references to Appendices
G 14 b Central (Nr POPERINGHE)	25.5.17 to 31.5.17		May 1917 (continued)	

Many Supplies stores being held for Issue to Divisions on a special distribution to the pm later by Q Branch. Such as Yukon Packs, Packsaddles S.S. Wirecutters. The special water carriers or racks which carry four petrol tins handed over in the 1st Corps have all to be made again but without any straps because the tins to to the pack. There are going to be made out of old canvas on the boot machines being brought out for an at the same time. Ration Sacks to be here kept up to 220 Sets (3 sacks going to a Set). It has been decided to take in the 2nd Blanket for 17th I. Brigade less any they care to return up to 25%. They are being stored tallied in a field behind the store. The rainless people cannot take them very rapidly on account of the want of trucks to Proven.

A general review being made of all outstanding indents & every effort being made to get free Franching from stores together with all important stores.

Since material is not allways like purchased in France great trouble is being found in connection with the Special colonies armbands that are to be supplied urgently for the Infantry. Salvage runners matters up etc. The base went to 5th Army base but they state that will not he ably to for a certain time which is too late for the first of June that are required.

A special rifle grenade carrier is also being locally made up for the division. The material required being a small stock of bread & leather canvas. The canvas of the cloth bales is being used for this. W.N. 34/1754 20,000. 5/15 D&D & L. A.D.S.S./Forms/C.2118. 15 (7)st Suppl: and broken up & the 188 p. battalion required

J. T. S [signature]
Capt [signature]

No 21

War Diary
Lieut A.J. Bowles.
h aod. So. 36. 6/1917
from 15/6/1917

To be forwarded in
paad. 2d. Divi-
by the 7th of the month
following. No A/1/1899
See

D.A.A.G.
    24th Division.

Herewith my War Diary for month
of June. 1917.

                N. F. Dodds. Lieut.
                        D.A.D.O.S.
                            24th Division

30/6/1917.

WAR DIARY or **INTELLIGENCE SUMMARY**

Army Form C. 2118.

Place: SHEET 28 G.26.C. Central

Date	Hour	Summary of Events and Information	Remarks
1.6.17		K.A.O.D. 30th Division. 2nd Corps com't up. Hinds that depot is just inside (by 100 yds) new area of theirs. 30th Division request that 30 huts go to look for a suitable site in the Reserve Divisional Area west of RENINGHELST toward BOESCHEPPE. No suitable buildings in the area at all — only an open field into which stores + a Marquee could be pitched. This was found 2½ kilo west of RENINGHELST. Railhead changed to this later place. Began to move leaving all the Divisional Blankets to be sent to rather from the old Store, with 1 Store tent & a marquee for office. Soon settling down. Weather extremely hot + rather difficult to keep Office work going under the great strain of it under canvas. Clerks finding it v. much.	
5.6.17 to 9.6.17		The list for move of all the special stores now sent out by "Q" treats everything was to go out on the following day which mean loading out the lorries to Brigade. Great trouble being experienced with regard to the special packs which HAZEBROUCK R.E. were not allowed to move to the last minute to this division. 10th Corps R.E. Park were given 2 days to make all their cards, but in spite of great efforts them material electric drills etc. Their effort was not a great success. However HAZEBROUCK were now allowed to issue 100 sets out of 240 required to a little later, more were	

WAR DIARY or INTELLIGENCE SUMMARY

Army Form C. 2118.

Place	Date	Hour	Summary of Events and Information	Remarks and references to Appendices
SASD ¼ Div own	June 1917 (continued)			
	5.6.17 to 9.6.17		Recruits from them finally the division was just brought up to strength. The Bootmakers had to work two whole nights on the straps/putting in eyelets, & Tailors making the straps on Serving machines. Frisker finished nicely each loose end to the rack. The employment of these men together with the Armourer at SASD Stos when located permits has proved on several occasions of great practical value in the manufacture of small items needed in great hast in the Sport. The division at the stage on paper was equipped with all its requirements — In connection with 'Shorts' for the men in Summer. It would be greatly to the advantage of the Service from an economical point of view as well as to the general satisfaction of Issuing Officers take those Serving these articles of Shorts were recognised as a Summer form of clothing & came up from the Base cheaply cut down. At present orders are issued that only the old trousers are to be cut down, but this is not the case. Many yards of	
	9.6.17		Potakis New Tomicade Cloth is wasted in order that trousers of Battalion may be alike. The waste water was but process is too long for O.C. of Battalion. — JHO S Contracts Pleodes was Sent down to the Base + Lt Dorleo ADS is carrying on in my Stead —	J.H.O. Murray Capt. SASD ¼ Div own

WAR DIARY
or
INTELLIGENCE SUMMARY

Army Form C. 2118.

Place	Date	Hour	Summary of Events and Information	Remarks and references to Appendices
	1917			
RENINGHELST (Sheet 27.S.W. C.5.1.4.)	10/6.	3.P.M.	Left X Corps Headquarters, accompanied by Lt. Col. Stone A.D.O.S., and proceeded to 24th Divisional HQrs where I was introduced to the A.A.& Q.M.G. (Col. Boyle) upon taking up my duties temporarily as D.A.D.O.S. in the absence of Capt. Sheppard. A.D.O. whose was admitted to Hospital this afternoon. Col. Stone took me to the Divisional Ordnance Dump, and he then returned to Corps HQrs: leaving me to carry on.	
	11/6.	9 A.m. & 7 P.M.	I interviewed the A.A. rQMG. at Div HQrs and discussed questions of collection and delivery of stores from Ordnance Dump to Units by Divisional train Transport instead of by lorry. Also the impending move of the Division to another area adjacent, and the selection of a fresh ordnance dump. Visited A.D.O.S. X Corps, & obtained authority for opening an Imprest A/c. in my name for the local purchase disbursements. Opened an A/c. at Field Cashier, X Corps (ABEELE) and drew 500 francs. Called at Railhead and interviewed O.O. X Corps Troops. Went to Bailleul to purchase special Singer Boot machine needles.	
		2h.m. onwards	Work in office and Store.	
	12-6	9.15 A.M.	Visited A.A. rQMG. and discussed question of move of Divisional HQs to a forward area, and the selection of a new site for Ordnance Depot, in the neighbourhood of K------- (MICMAC CAMP).	
		2.P.M. & 7.30 P.M.	Visited ADOS. X Corps in regard to a suggested improvement in the method of cleaning the Gas cylinder of Lewis Machine gun, by doing away with the Cleaning Rod and substituting a Pull through.	

Army Form C. 2118.

WAR DIARY
or
INTELLIGENCE SUMMARY.
(Erase heading not required.)

Instructions regarding War Diaries and Intelligence Summaries are contained in F.S. Regs., Part II. and the Staff Manual respectively. Title pages will be prepared in manuscript.

Place	Date	Hour	Summary of Events and Information	Remarks and references to Appendices
RENINGHELST (Sheet 27. 9.33. a.5.4.)	12-6 (Contd)		Went to Hagebrouck, Merville, and Bailleul, and interviewed Civilian tradesmen in regard to local purchase transactions previously made by Capt. Sheppard, the former D.A.D.O.S., and made arrangements as to the completion of orders. Principally the making of canvas haversacks for rifle grenades.	
	13-6		Lieut. Waters. A.D.B. Assistant Inspector of Armaments (2nd Army) arrived at Depôt, and inspected Armourers Shop. I went out and selected the site for the new depôt and made preliminary arrangements for moving. The map reference of the new site is Sheet 28. N.I. central, and we are now in a position within easy reach of Divl. H.Qrs and also the H.Qrs of Brigades, which will facilitate the receipt and disposal of both new and old Ordnance stores. We are also commencing to use a more advanced Railhead at Ouderdom for drawing supplies, but at present all old and other stores for despatch to Base are being sent to Reninghelst Railhead.	
Sheet 28. N.I. Central	14-6		Commenced to move camp to new site (N.I. central.) By this evening we had shifted about half the stores in the Depôt. Lieut Waters. A.D.B. A.D.A. left this afternoon and proceeded to the Ordnance Depôt of the 23rd Division at Berthem.	
	15-6		Continued moving camp all day. The issue of stores to the Division proceeded just the same, and everything was issued to Brigades this afternoon from the new dump.	
	16-6		Finished clearing the old Depôt, and continued erecting covered huts for stores.	

WAR DIARY
or
INTELLIGENCE SUMMARY.

(Erase heading not required.)

Army Form C. 2118.

Place	Date	Hour	Summary of Events and Information	Remarks and references to Appendices
Sheet 28 M.I central	16-6 (contd)		Went to 2nd Army School of Sniping, and obtained six rifles with telescopic sights, which had been repaired and overhauled. Called at Corps H.Q'rs and interviewed A.D.O.S. re Army Field Artillery Brigades attached to this Division, also called at X Corps Ordnance Mobile Workshops about Generators under repair.	
	17-6.		Visited Divisional Headquarters in the morning, and spent remainder of the day in the depôt going into the question of the amount of Stores on hand, and accommodation of them. Work in office.	
	18-6.		Called at Corps H.Q'rs and discussed with A.D.O.S. the question of the defects continually being found in Lewis Machine Guns and Magazines sent out from England. The matter has today been referred to Army with a view to steps being taken to trace the name of the makers, and remedy the defects.	
	19-6.		Interviewed two Belgian farmers and fixed terms for the hire of two meadows used for Ordnance Depôt. Took Interpreter from Belgian Mission attached to Div. H.Q'rs with me. Settled for 10½ frs. for 2 weeks. Went to Dunkerque to purchase parts for Boot Repairing machine which was otherwise unusable.	
	20.6		Called on the Mayor of Westoutre and obtained his signature on the Army forms for the payment to the two Belgian Farmers for hire of meadows for Sept. This afternoon I spent going into the question of the underclothing and other articles required to equip a Divisional Laundry about to be opened at Dickebusch, and general office routine.	

Army Form C. 2118.

WAR DIARY
or
INTELLIGENCE SUMMARY.
(Erase heading not required.)

Instructions regarding War Diaries and Intelligence Summaries are contained in F. S. Regs., Part II. and the Staff Manual respectively. Title pages will be prepared in manuscript.

Place	Date	Hour	Summary of Events and Information	Remarks and references to Appendices
Sheet 28 N.I. Central	21-6		Called at Divisional Headquarters and discussed question of return by Units of the special stores used in recent operations, and which will not be required in the rest area, and the method of disposal of same. Visited Corps H.Qrs and O.O. I Corps. Shops. Daily office routine.	
	22-6		Daily office routine, and preparations for the refitting of the Division on coming out of the line shortly.	
	23-6		Called on D.A.m. I Corps and left some artillery instruments, and binoculars for repair. Called on D.A.D.O.S. 23rd and 47th Divisions, and made arrangements in connection with the move of the Division (49th) to a rest area, and the administration of the Units remaining behind. Took stock of depot equipment.	
	24-6		Visited A.D.O.S. and O.O. I Corps, and arranged for the hire of a building for the storage of divisional stores and equipment not required in the rest area, and commenced to move the stores by lorry. Discussed with D.A.D.O.S. 23rd Division, question of what canvas accommodation I was prepared to leave behind on handing over Depot site to him. Daily Office routine. Paid N.C.O.'s and men.	
	25-6		Daily office routine. Visited several tradesmen and paid accounts for local purchase. Continued to transfer stores from the depot to the Divisional Store in Pheale, and generally prepared for move into the Rest area.	
	26-6		Daily office routine. Went to Divisional Headquarters and conferred with D.A.Q.M.G. on the question of the provision for sanitary arrangements in rest area, and of refitting the Division.	

Army Form C. 2118.

WAR DIARY
or
INTELLIGENCE SUMMARY.
(Erase heading not required.)

Instructions regarding War Diaries and Intelligence Summaries are contained in F. S. Regs., Part II. and the Staff Manual respectively. Title pages will be prepared in manuscript.

Place	Date	Hour	Summary of Events and Information	Remarks and references to Appendices
Sheet 28. N.I. Central.	27-6		Daily office routine. Made final preparations for moving the Depôt to the new area. Despatched two lorries and some men as advance party, and certain stores. Arranged for the ordnance stores to be delivered to the Artillery units to remaining behind, and made provision for supply of anti-gas appliances for refitting the Artillery &c.	
Lumbres	28-6		Completed moving Depôt to Lumbres, and handed over to D.A.D.O.S. 23rd Division. Leakage at the old depôt at N.I. Central.	
	29-6		Daily office routine. Spent rest of day arranging details of new Depôt. Capt. Sheppard D.A.D.O.S. returned from sick leave.	
	30-6		Daily office routine. Spent the day handing over papers and documents to Capt. Sheppard, balancing Imprest Account &c.	

A. J. Dodds Lieut.
D.A.D.O.S.
24th Division.

30/6/1917.

14

D.A.S.
3rd Echelon

Herewith my War
Diary for July 1917

Jno. Sherran
Capt DADOS
nz Div:

11/8/17

WAR DIARY or INTELLIGENCE SUMMARY

Army Form C. 2118

Place	Date	Hour	Summary of Events and Information	Remarks and references to Appendices
LUMBRES	1-7-17		Returned to Division on 29th June. Took over again from Lt DODDS, who is going on leave tomorrow - No reliefs yet fixed for A.D.). Stores at No BAILLEUL has been signed 30 to 35 miles away - & no one at war. 10th & 4th on rail - notified for Race - Gunners & No 1 Cay Train also Motor Sec September 23rd Division - Thought wk for a few days - Units in a very large area - extreme west only 12 miles from BOULOGNE. While R.E. are central units BLARINGHEM area S.E. of Saint Omer - Units begin to settle down - have been badly knocked about & require another for refit. Stores the new unit to 71st IB at NABRINGHEM, 72nd COLUMBY, 73rd - Come in time. R.E. being sent out every 3rd day. Gunners will have the Sect out where they are transport'd. Sim Park delivers Stores each Wednesday.	
	2-7-17		To ST OMER to see ADRT to find out where Stores ahead leaving Calais had been sent - finally it was discovered from him that those to BAILLEUL. Saw A.D.O.S. L.of.C. not arranged with him about TRAFFIC HAZEBROUCK to LUMBRES. Got Stores sent without further to LUMBRES - 3 LORRIES dispatches to MERVILLE to fix bicc for several unfortunate Stores obtained prior to fight East time division were up.	

Army Form C. 2118.

WAR DIARY
or
INTELLIGENCE SUMMARY.

(Erase heading not required.)

Place	Date	Hour	Summary of Events and Information	Remarks and references to Appendices
LUMBRES			July 1917 (continued)	LADD 74 Div -
	3.7.17 & 4.7.17		Stores received from BAILLEUL. Heard at h'ts R.Points - lorries great trouble is the distance lorries are going wrong -	(HD)
	5.7.17		First day stores received from LUMBRES arrived. Postern much better.	(HD)
	6.7.17		To STOMER talked for rifle magnets - TO WAR II RECQUES to see Staff Captain RA. found he was urgently requiring 40 tents, washing bowls, & underclothing as gunners first coming out of this area. This was all arranged. Their sent on RA + RE lorry to their R.Point tomorrow. TO CASSEL to DDOS as to whether fur Park is going or not from Second Army. DDOS said it was moving from 6pm today to Fifth Army - Transferring all demands from them to base except field guns & carriages which would automatically be transferred to base.	(HD)
	7.7.17		Large issue of clothing ate going out. Four lorry loads sent out to RA + RE. Units generally needing a lot of equipment.	(HD)
	8.7.17		Weather very much cooler the last few days. Issues as usual	(HD)
	9.7.17		Sent 6½ tents down to LE CHATELET for 7 + 18. - Parts of their men being sent to the sea. Issues as usual to 17 R.Point + RE + RA - 135 rifles the Canyards collected for Armourer Shop to now to divisions. Many required. NoID Hospital STOMER supplies these material for making up rifle grenades. Forenoon. Plays for Signals. To MERVILLE H2216	(HD)

Army Form C. 2118.

WAR DIARY
or
INTELLIGENCE SUMMARY.
(Erase heading not required.)

Instructions regarding War Diaries and Intelligence Summaries are contained in F. S. Regs., Part II. and the Staff Manual respectively. Title pages will be prepared in manuscript.

Place	Date	Hour	Summary of Events and Information	Remarks and references to Appendices
LUMBRES	10.7.17		July 1917 (continued) A.D.S.S. 9/4th Division. 73 I.B. party have to return from LE CHATELET, have a look Lat to So down here again today. to trial back the 64 tents. Lewis' out to 17 I.B. on same lorry. takes the RATRE R.Point. (M.D.)	
	11.7.17		To STOMER & rifles & local purchase, went onto AIRE & find a store which might be required for summer if the Div is to be railheaded. Saw R.T.O. who said he could arrange for store. Div trams to LUMBRES. The reason they would to move Div — to AIRE is due to the fact that 2nd Portuguese Division is moving there & 34th Div A.O.Q. is on Perne Section label. To MERVILLE to Sachs for rifle grenade carriers. To GODEWAERSVELDE to arrange transport of stores to 5th Army Sun Park. (M.D.)	
	12.7.17		No stores to railhead. Nother sent out to R.Points. An new recirculated (M.D.)	
	13.7.17		Stores received at LUMBRES again. No lorry sent out to R.points. Pioneers have moved up to STEENVOORDE. Stores being sent them on RATRE lorry which is also sent to pick up stores from Sun Park (M.D.)	
	14.7.17		No stores from railhead — No lorries sent out. (M.D.)	
	15.7.17		Large number of stores up at railhead — Lewis out to 17 I.B. & stores to 153 F.Co. who are up towards the line & Lewis & 100 wearing boots being taken from Guards. G.D. Camieff. Stores being sent out to Gunners at RENINGHELST. Lorry called back at Sun Park for stores (M.D.)	
	16.7.17			

Army Form C. 2118.

WAR DIARY
or
INTELLIGENCE SUMMARY.
(Erase heading not required.)

Instructions regarding War Diaries and Intelligence Summaries are contained in F. S. Regs., Part II. and the Staff Manual respectively. Title pages will be prepared in manuscript.

Place	Date	Hour	Summary of Events and Information	Remarks and references to Appendices
LUMBRES	July 1917 (continued)		D.A.D.O.S. 74th Division	
	17.7.17		17 IB convoi in to LUMBRES & 72 Sonj towards 1st line – H.Q. of Division moving to STEENVOORGT on 19/7/17 for a few days before going on to ZEVECOTEN. Arranged tomorrow A.O.S. straight here to either one of the 2 Ordnance stores in RENINGHELST or tents at ZEVECOTEN. All special stores such as wirecutters etc being taken over there. Stores were yesterday drawn from V Army Gun Park those for A Kitchen were run into RENINGHELST together with those from here drawn in 23rd Division stores there. Suspended all stores to come from Base today until after the move. Went yesterday to see A.D.O.S. 23rd Division, POPERINGHE to settle little + back after seeing A.D.O.S. II Corps & D.	
	18.7.17		To AIRE railhead – no more trucks to be received to LUMBRES – to MERVILLE for rifle grenade carriers, brought back 4,80 –. Issue falling off as units beginning to move.	J + D
	19.7.17		Stores at RENINGHELST promised by II Corps. Sent up R.A. Stores, dental kit J+D for other units not necessary yet as they are still moving.	

2353 Wt W2541/1454 700,000 5/15 D D & L A.D.S.S/Forms/C. 2118.

Army Form C. 2118.

WAR DIARY
or
INTELLIGENCE SUMMARY.
(Erase heading not required.)

Instructions regarding War Diaries and Intelligence Summaries are contained in F. S. Regs., Part II. and the Staff Manual respectively. Title pages will be prepared in manuscript.

Place	Date	Hour	Summary of Events and Information	Remarks and references to Appendices
			DADOS 24th Division	
LUMBRES	20.7.17 & 21.7.17		July 1917 (continued) Removed suspension on Base. Cleaning Stores as fast as possible. Still keeping up issues to R.A.	(Itd)
RENINGHELST	22.7.17 to 31.7.17		Came up to RENINGHELST with remainder of Stores & office. Enormous quantities of Special Stores the issues to be made as soon as possible. Pack Saddles, Yukon packs, ration carriers, water carriers, wirecutters, trench stores etc all being issued as quickly as possible under a special distribution. Magneta Cartridges for the whole division being supplied by V Army (DADOS).	(Itd)

J.H.D Sherrars
Capt DADOS 24th Division

2353 Wt. W 2541/1454 700,000 5/15 D. D. & L. A.D.S.S./Forms/C. 2118.

WAR DIARY or INTELLIGENCE SUMMARY

Army Form C. 2118.

96/23

Place	Date	Hour	Summary of Events and Information	Remarks and references to Appendices
G35 G.4.9. RENINGHELST to OUDERDOM ROAD	1.8.17 to 11.8.17		August 1917. BASS 24th Division. Pitched out of store which had just been set into by 30th Division who states they must have it. This being done after having previously encountered 3 days before. This a most important time when reinforcements return are being made - Finally had to let into 4 to 20 men huts in a field where no tent were to be put up - Pouring rain on morning of arrival. At these sites guards be gone into by Corps who can help Commanders where troops are in such a encountered condition. It is not right to have to hustle stores down anywhere as a moments notice when it is not really necessary. Weather, leaving, & change & continuous rain starting. Tremendous inconvenience of clothing required to fix up the men after the first two days of this offensive. Sent down 5 lorries to Calais Base thought back approx. 3000 suits. We returned clothes coming back here via batts. after being disinfected, baths etc. Tailors heading up what can be done here & clothing not good for return. Sewing machines recently purchased for tailors not useful in this work. For quantities of stores have also been sent. (in)	

Army Form C. 2118.

WAR DIARY
or
INTELLIGENCE SUMMARY.
(Erase heading not required.)

Place	Date	Hour	Summary of Events and Information	Remarks and references to Appendices
			D.A.D.O.S. 24th Division	
G.35.b.4.9	12.8.17 to 17.8.17		August 1917 (continued) Much enemy bombing going on most nights & shelling at various intervals. A few have fallen in the field in which depot is & several more round about near the railway which runs each side of this location. Stores coming up & repairs from Base as far as days allotted so. One has this is due to truck shortage the big quantities of ammunition which of course come first. Owing to the sudden great speed of weather those coming back, in spite of having been disinfected. Most of the returned clothing coming back, in spite of having been disinfected. Hooked this through by Tailors specially put in for the work, could not be reused. Into too has a state. D.A.D.O.S. 56th Division doing duty for me while I go on leave – (JHO)	
	28.8.17		Returned from leave to find less than 2 men were killed & 2 wounded from the Australian & 23rd Division Artillery Staffs attached – This was due to bombs. Most of the special stores (packsaddles etc.) recently issued to being returned by units as they require it no longer. Routine work as usual.	

J.H.Sheppard
Capt. D.A.D.O.S
24th Division

WAR DIARY or INTELLIGENCE SUMMARY

Army Form C. 2118.

D.A.D.O.S.
24 Div

Army Form C. 2118.

WAR DIARY
or
INTELLIGENCE SUMMARY.
(Erase heading not required.)

Instructions regarding War Diaries and Intelligence Summaries are contained in F. S. Regs., Part II. and the Staff Manual respectively. Title pages will be prepared in manuscript.

Place	Date	Hour	Summary of Events and Information	Remarks and references to Appendices
			September 1917	A.D.O.S. 74th Division
G35 b-4-9	1.9.17		To ADOS & field cashier - went into railhead. Floral procession.	
RENINGHELST	2.9.17		Clear moonlight in the evening. Many enemy aeroplanes over. Bombs dropped on store. One hit one of the buildings setting it on fire - there was petrol, underwear,	
OUDERDOM				
Reny			what not and dropped also liking. Means had to set down to their duty out, consequently fire got out of control. When it was safe to come out every effort was made to get the fire out. Apart from many cases with ammunition (rocket) made a long time to the nearest pond some 250 yards away, and hustle up water. It was further got underground by 1 am that also in spite of normal until morning 2000£ worth of stocks were destroyed. Ordinary routine followed. A fresh marquee was obtained for the stores to make	
	3.9.17 to			
	11.9.17		up to 2 huts that were destroyed. Oil antigas apparatus forward. Events telling. near launch	(A2)
	12.9.17		Acting for Col. Duckett Lt. Poldwin went to Base (Calais) having been given a commission in the Tank Corps.	(A2)
	13.9.17 to 15.9.17		Weather stale & clear at night - few raids - much hostile bombing near store.	
			Head of Division moved to MERRIS out from his Hippo along to Second Army	(A2)
MERRIS	16.9.17		Moved in same hired Renault to MERRIS having handed over all apparatus etc to 23rd Staff (A2)
	17.9.17	19.47	Bureau moved to IV Corps - Matthew Army Rear Battle Formation - Received no stores to minimum	
			amount for a trek force ammunition Northern Heavy Kit on by rail	
BEUGNY	20.9.17		Division H.Q. here for a few days before pursuit into III Corps- Established office &	
HAPLINCOURT			Small store with a portion of Ammunition Shop for any urgent requirements	(A2)
ROAD				

WAR DIARY or INTELLIGENCE SUMMARY

Army Form C. 2118.

Place	Date	Hour	Summary of Events and Information	Remarks and references to Appendices
BEUGNY	27.9.17		September (continued)	
HAPLINCOURT ROAD	28.9.17		To new area NOBESCOURT FARM - Saw RADOS RADOS 34th Division from whom Several Stores were taken over - He only had tents and accommodation & handcarts. Whatsoe, with the exception of an Adrian Hut lying in pieces on ground - found that all stores are sent by IBECAUVILLE (light rail) that only one lorry is left with RADOS. Sent on Armourer, Bootmakers, Tailors has many stores gradually to bonfire - deposits on the huts (bridges) where the Armourers got orders. Auto of 4 type have been found. Men arriving. Men are of little use here being bootless. Adrian Huts have been demanded (1st blanket only). Are blanket of Horse Hugs have been demanded (1st blanket only) JHS	
NOBESCOURT FARM	29.9.17		Moved to NOBESCOURT FARM dump with Office & remaining Stores. ADRIAN HUT together with 2 4/2 but a bit work, most of the nails for both Marquee were parcelled to railway the huts in best powder for same. The siding for ORTHANES is now being put in. To kit presnt see steen toffie in Marquee. A flight of steps to be made on either side of ramp. Item made of an stanch stores any. Ammn trader a trick road on either side of ramp JHS	
	30.9.17			

J.H.S. Sussex
Capt RADO 39th Divn

D.A.S., Office
Base

Herewith War Diary for DADOS 24 Division for month of
October 1917.

J. H. S. Skinner
Capt. DADOS
24 Division

[stamp: D.AD.O.S. 24th DIVISION. No...... Date......]

WAR DIARY or INTELLIGENCE SUMMARY

Army Form C. 2118.

DADOS 24 Div
Vol 25

S.A.D.O.S. 24 Division

Place	Date	Hour	Summary of Events and Information	Remarks and references to Appendices
NOBESCOURT FARM	October 1917			
	1.10.17 to		Great amount of constructional work having been done by the detachment, it is able to maintain deliveries now being received nearly work & heavy.	
	7.10.17 to		Rain started. Swamped out of Marquee. Nissen hut being erected to office with aid of my sapper. Advisable that this going on gradually. All flannel cloth mackintosh have been mixed.	
	17.10.17		Slight detail in Quartermaster's have begun to obtain warm handlers from 34 Division. Review quickly with Hare as to who is going to met clothing demands. Considerable delay caused thereby. Owners mixed breeds are days bulk demand for clothes altogether. The demand being about to this week. Executive dummy telephone some, but cross in yard and at ROISEL (quickly) not v satisfactory at present. Arrange with M.A.T.O.R.C. to 3 Column Supply Centre to load trains at ROISEL (m). Keep one N.C.C. representative & Railways to check stores generally look after our railed work.	

Army Form C. 2118.

WAR DIARY
or
INTELLIGENCE SUMMARY.
(Erase heading not required.)

Instructions regarding War Diaries and Intelligence Summaries are contained in F. S. Regs., Part II. and the Staff Manual respectively. Title pages will be prepared in manuscript.

Place	Date	Hour	Summary of Events and Information	Remarks and references to Appendices
	October 1917 (continued)		A.D.M.S. 24th Division	
NOBESCOURT FARM	18.10.17		Winter clothing has commenced to arrive with the exception of jerkins & goats [illegible] [illegible]	
K.31 central Map 62c	19.10.17 to 31.10.17		Setting our shelter onto an accommodation and [illegible] than potato huts. This however is not sufficient for all purposes. Canteen is starting owing to the great difficulty of obtaining any stores for the men — The C.R.E. has been asked for 7 men [illegible] of another Adrian Hut. M.O. Irwin (acting for [illegible]) has been posted from [illegible] [illegible] Troops to take over duties of R.M.O. in place of Red Cross to Poitiers who went to Cie Calais after receiving a Commission. Stores coming up quite well from France. Gum Boots are arriving. Good pairs of [illegible] the 1st Issue to be more than are really [illegible] by K.R. Swam [illegible]. Consequently reissues are being carried out A.D.J. furnished [illegible] Slips started with 3 men of there many would be full in ten [illegible] [illegible] to the hope was [illegible]. Epidemic of PUO's has been fairly heavy on the Divisional Area of [illegible] [illegible]. Weather begins to become [illegible] and roads round depot require a great deal of attention to prevent [illegible] falling in.	

J.H. Stephens
Capt. A.D.M.S. 24th Division

> D.A.D.O.S.,
> 24th
> DIVISION.
>
> No............
> Date..........

D.A.S.
3rd Echelon
Base

Herewith my war
Diaries for November
1917.

J.H.D. Sheppard. CAPT.
D.A.D.O.S., 24th DIVISION

1/12/17

WAR DIARY or INTELLIGENCE SUMMARY

Army Form C-2118.

DADOS 24D Div Nov 26

Place	Date	Hour	Summary of Events and Information	Remarks and references to Appendices
NOBESCOURT FARM K.33 central Map 62 C	1.11.17 to 10.11.17		November 1917. Supervision stops being taken daily to the elementary units of Broken Guns. Mosquito BMS Cops are now found. Potable water fixed for Boot Reps as tAmmunn Reps have paid quite a reasonable proof of the Studies were to work, but have been strengthened since the results have been quite good.	
	11.11.17 to 25.11.17		N.C. Containers on demand for the whole division. Two thousand reserve sets of Service Dress (Jackets Trousers) have been issued to the Divisional Substance — 650 of each being sent to each Brigade, leaving 200 regs to W.O.I. Store. Leather Jerkins for Pioneers & Indian Ratalian not available. Weather alternately between mild & wet with much wind. The registered number of all Lewis Guns with Division now being recorded. Whenever a new gun is issued the No. of same it is replacing is taken out of book therein inserted. It has been found that the 6000 Guns books are now more than at present required — 2000 of those still awaiting issue at the Store.	

Army Form C. 2118.

WAR DIARY
or
INTELLIGENCE SUMMARY.
(Erase heading not required.)

Instructions regarding War Diaries and Intelligence Summaries are contained in F. S. Regs., Part II. and the Staff Manual respectively. Title pages will be prepared in manuscript.

Place	Date	Hour	Summary of Events and Information	Remarks and references to Appendices
			ADSS 24th Division	
NOBESCOURT FARM. K 33 central Map 62C	November 1917 (continued) 26.XI.17 to 30.XI.17		The Second Clipper Machines are now returning with firing units. Benthoff to M.T. Base. The Divisional Reserves of M.G. Ammn are up their exchanged as rapidly as possible. Warning Order issued for a move, but this is now suspended due to a sudden enemy attack, so that at present the Division remains where it is. New half 100ft Adnew shot now issued for M.G. gunners canvass ammunition. Reported loss of A.107 18½ five pieces but not yet confirmed if New guns are required.	

J.H.S. Shepart
Capt ADSS 24 Division

D.A.G.,
   3rd Echelon,
      Base.

Herewith my War Diary for

the month of December 1917,

J.H.D. Sheppard
                    CAPT.
D.A.D.O.S., 24th DIVISION

24

Army Form C. 2118.

Vol 27

WAR DIARY
or
INTELLIGENCE SUMMARY.
(Erase heading not required.)

SAOS ret-Division

Instructions regarding War Diaries and Intelligence Summaries are contained in F. S. Regs., Part II. and the Staff Manual respectively. Title pages will be prepared in manuscript.

Place	Date	Hour	Summary of Events and Information	Remarks and references to Appendices
NORSESCARPT FARM	1·12·17		G.S. boots extremely bad this turn. All last b'ttle alarms before they could be worn & even now are proving to be most unsatisfactory —	
K. 33 Central 62C. Map	2·12·17 to		Visit from A.D.O.P. Stores coming up quite well, altho great shortage of Electric Torch bulbs, and Chevrons.	M2
	7·12·17		Men sent up to replace 'A' Storeman are turning out very well. These Storesmen quite fit for this work. Needed repairs turn to turn a cors time series of hours.	M2
	8·12·17 to		Pickets firm reads all complied with. Elevating dials in Armour shop. Being taken out by Cavalry Corps trans. K A.D.O.P. not at present having any O.O. Cap't Troops several extra units being taken on for Ordnance Service by this Division. The 3rd Cavalry Dismounted Brigade and 4th R.H.Artillery being the largest amount among the number. Large number of most items due out to these units who seem the very short trucking. A lot of looting after.	M2
	20·12·17		Heavy snow fall. Several inches, most transport hung up. Great demand for Frost Cogs & trap leather nails. Most of the cargo were areirles of a certain number of nails, but on the whole the Division has done well on the point.	

Army Form C. 2118.

WAR DIARY
or
INTELLIGENCE SUMMARY.
(Erase heading not required.)

Place	Date	Hour	Summary of Events and Information	Remarks and references to Appendices
MOEUVRES COURT FARM	26.12.17 to		December 1917 (continued)	D.A.D.O.S. 24th Division
Kyzencourt Map 62c	31.12.17		Answers have been obtained to demands made on the rest of the Services required by the Division. These are now all on demand.	
			It is pointed out how very unsatisfactory the system of getting Divisional armourers the repairs thro' the workshops is. Frequently the work could be done with divison of a APF. artificer Armourer, two other men were added to the Divisional Armourer Shop. For example the frame of rifles with chambers could easily be done and the number broken is large taking often a long time to be done at the I.O.M.S. Shop, especially when there is a big pressure of gun work there. The work in Armourers shops has been got well under way lately. Many cycles having passed thro' the numbers to repair greatly diminished. This may partly be due to the associated armourers who have been recently trained in Armourer forge work. They exist have it is too late — weather still very severe. —	
			Stock (reserve) of Clothing has proved most useful this expiring stores always be late. —	
			Men are getting their leave much more regularly now —	

J.M.S. Peppard
Capt. D.A.D.O.S.
24th Division

D.A.G.,
Third Echelon.

      Herewith War Diaries for the months of January, February and March 1918.
      Delay in forwarding same, is much regretted.

The remainder to date are being forwarded in a few days-

J.W.D.Shepherd

23/6/18.
                      Major, D.A.D.O.S.,
                      24th Division.

WAR DIARY
or
INTELLIGENCE SUMMARY.

Army Form C. 2118.

(Erase heading not required.)

MADOS 24th DIV FD
Jan Feb March

Vols 28, 29, 30

Place	Date	Hour	Summary of Events and Information	Remarks and references to Appendices
NOBESCOURT FARM	1-1-18		January 1918	
			Weather v. cold. Visited by ADS. during the period. Stores working well by the Greenville system. From	
MESCOURT	5-1-18		ROISSEL to the depot. Convoys have always required to prevent stores falling from trucks.	
62C (Map)			Div Supply Column Loaders supply all labour needed transport stores from Brono to Greenville Rail.	
	6-1-18 to 13-1-18		Depot becoming v. complete. Tempest huts have proved to be well placed round the Greenville line making loading unloading very simple. The road on opposite side of line getting v. bad from which to take an the vehicles waiting to draw stores. Quantities of wire (loose) from the broken down villages round have been used for this. The two portable huts comprising the boot shop & armourers shop that is in use proves to be the most successful. The arrangement of straw between 2 skins of canvas makes a v. warm shop. The outside canvas being laced sheet form the roof on a light portable structure.	
	14-1-18 to 28-1-18		Went on leave	
	29.6.31		It has been decided that the ADSs as [an officer] of ?? representative should remain in station in order to make all arrangements for & attach from them with the Division of same or from that.	FD1. FD2.

F.H.S. Shepperd.
Capt. SASOS. 24th Division

Army Form C. 2118.

WAR DIARY
or
INTELLIGENCE SUMMARY
(Erase heading not required.)

Instructions regarding War Diaries and Intelligence Summaries are contained in F. S. Regs., Part II. and the Staff Manual respectively. Title pages will be prepared in manuscript.

Place	Date	Hour	Summary of Events and Information	Remarks and references to Appendices
MOBECOURT FARM K33 central Map 62c	1.2.18 to 15.2.18		February 1918 — A Cavalry Dismounted Brigade has been working with the Division for some periods this Kui Ordnance Stores have been supplied from this depot. Staff under Cavalry Corps. 191st Machine Gun Coy. recently had to fit a section of 4 guns complete with personnel to Eygpt. They had to be hurriedly equipped from other Coys when necessary with all their outstanding demands.	S.A.D.O.S. 2nd Division
	16.2.18		The question of a motor car or box car for S.A.D.O.S. At this time has been very much felt. The much needed car (which has now been evacuated to S.A.D.O.S.) that if sick to divisions all cars, including S.A.D.O.S. can be posted in State of S.A.D.O.S. having first claim from the pool is nothing — no amount of "first claim" is any good if S.A.D.O.S. journey requires a car at say 3 o'clock in the afternoon and they are all out when applied for.	S.A.D.O.S
	17.2.18 to 28.2.18		The Pioneers are losing a Coy, this reduces a good deal of equipment including 2 Lewis guns. These have all been returned to stores. One Battalion in each Brigade is being disbanded. 8th Buffs — 2nd Kensingtons — 12 Yorkshires All their equipment came in well then have been returned to the Base. Their Regimental Transport has been left in the Division one with each Brigade.	S.A.D.O.S

J.M.D. Shepherd
Capt. S.A.D.O.S 2nd Division

Army Form C. 2118.

WAR DIARY
or
INTELLIGENCE SUMMARY.
(Erase heading not required.)

S.A.D.S. 24th Division

Place	Date	Hour	Summary of Events and Information	Remarks and references to Appendices
	March 1918			
NOBESCOURT FARM	1.3.18 to 4.3.18		The Machine Gun Corps are being amalgamated forming a M.Gun Battalion. Approval taste is all that has been supplied to date. No great increase of equipment. So ammo for Trench Mortars.	(JRD)
K33 central Map 62 c	5.3.18 to		Weather generally very bad. Orders have been received by 66th Division. Went to Flamincourt (Peronne).	
FLAMICOURT (PERONNE)	15.3.18		Petrol Nissen Hut for office. Store in a Stn tent nearby. Rations were sent out by lorry to which point was at LE CHATELET. All stores were sent out by lorry to which worked admirably.	
			Moved into 19th Corps. Rear Divisional H.Q. was at Flamicourt while advanced was further up at MERAUCOURT.	
			D.D.O.S. visits the depot. Weather improved considerably. All stores coming up well.	(JRD)
BOUVINCOURT	16.3.18 & 17.3.18		Division moving into BOUVINCOURT. I moved up the depot into tents there where we very soon got settled in.	
	18.3.18		A.D.O.S. decided I was to have 106" Newton Mortars pending further instructions. These Mortars had been returned by S.T.M.O. surplus to establishment - taken over again	(JRD)

WAR DIARY
or
INTELLIGENCE SUMMARY.

Army Form C. 2118.

Place	Date	Hour	Summary of Events and Information	Remarks and references to Appendices
	(Continued)		March 1918	ADDS 74th Division
SOUVINCOURT	18.3.18 (continued)		Question of A.A. defence guns, mounts, tripods became acute. Tank Section attached to Division. Provision of trench shelters for camouflage. Stripping of Depot Battn completed. Ascale of equipment for future units should be laid down per cent. All surplus stores removed to LA MOTTE when a suitable reserve Ordnance store had been taken.	J.M.D.
	19.3.18		ADDS left for eight days PARIS leave. Provision of extra stretchers, blankets toilet for Yellow Gas Patients.	J.M.D.
	20.3.18		Purchase of 5 barrels in AMIENS to be cut down into for use in Divisional Laundry for cleaning clothing contaminated with yellow Gas. Brigade asking for additional Very Light pistols.	J.M.D.
	21.3.18	5 a.m.	Depot heavily shelled. No real damage done. An tank removed from Camp up to 12 noon. Order to move received from "Q". 2 lorries taken to move Divisional H.Q. Commenced to move East of BRIE BRIDGE with one lorry up to 6 p.m. when the other two returned. Report question of disposal of attached units to ADDS.	J.M.D.

Army Form C. 2118.

WAR DIARY
or
INTELLIGENCE SUMMARY.
(Erase heading not required.)

DADOS 24th Division

March 1918 (Continued)

Place	Date	Hour	Summary of Events and Information	Remarks and references to Appendices
BRIE	22.3.18		More empties. Empty barrels & packages left behind, also quantity of old clothing. Bosch coming on fairly quickly.	
	23.3.18		Orders by "Q" to move to MARCHELPOT. Three lorries taken away by "Q" to convey ammunition to troops in the line. One lorry with 6" Mortars taken important stores sent on to MARCHELPOT first. Impossible to move more until 6pm. after reporting to Brigadier of RA who had a Group of Guns in action in rear of Ordnance Dump. M. Gun position taken up in Ordnance Dump. Jacates dump & all stores remaining after arrangements had been made with the R.A. Officer to his time before he withdrew. Forty men of detachment marched to MARCHELPOT. Reported to "Q" Orders & proceed to HULU. (near CHAULNES). Lorries returned. Railhead MARCHELPOT. No stores received. All stores carriers in Base & those subsequently received at R'Head were reconsigned to Base, who were notified of Division being on the move.	
	24.3.18		Sent motors to steam Mobile W.Shops. "Q" notified that stores has been abandoned. Left HULU for ROZIERS at 10.30 a.m. Reported to Army on route.	

WAR DIARY
or
INTELLIGENCE SUMMARY.

Army Form C. 2118.

Place	Date	Hour	Summary of Events and Information	Remarks and references to Appendices
			March 1918 (continued) BATOS in Sweden	
			17/B. applied for 40 Lewis Guns. 60 obtained from Gun Park & sent the 40 into the line -	
			90 issued. Various units en route. 17th/B. asked for 600 sets of equipment from Havrincourt - Equipment collected from C.C.S. & Haviens. O. decided blankets need not be carried. Railway not known. Gun Park moved to LONGEAU - issued 400 magazines Lewis Gun to 72nd I.B. - M.G.Bat'n supplied with 12 pans & 14 mounts - 73rd I.B supplied with 16 Guns + 500 magazines Lewis - GOYEUX IGNACOURT Road (MD)	
ROZIERS	25.3.18		16 Lewis Guns supplied to M. Gun Batt'n. 6 tripods traversing parts - 20 Lewis Guns supplied to 17th/B. 8 to 72nd - all with 44 magazines each. 6 testing Guns required by M.S. Batt'n amn Known no auxiliary mounts. 110 boxes of belt supplied to M.S. Batt'n also 6 spare part boxes. (MD)	
JEMUIN	26.3.18		Left ROZIERS midnight 25/3/18. Arrived JEMVIN 2 am 26/3/18. Remained Buffer Store from LA MOTTE & recollected BOVES - Shortage ammunition of rifle ???	
	27.3.18		Manche - Some obtained Haviers. 73rd/B. issued with 6 Lewis Guns + 500 magazines. Division coming back. - Issues of Guns & ?? - Ammunition orders to men. ????? ammunition back to AMIENS. Great difficulty in finding Division. Finally found them at CASTEL - store taken	
CASTEL	28.3.18		collected during 28/3/18 from ABBEVILLE trains same night. Reserve men & equipment handclothing fed.	
COTTENCHY	29.3.18 to 31.3.18		Proceeded to COTTENCHY in the dark. Lewis Gun Van taken in towing too much to proceed in any of three transports. The great object was to cope the rest of AILEY units as much as possible. JUNSE was used as a half-way house en route for COTTENCHY. ARRIVED at COTTENCHY 29/3/. Ref.Gu 5/15 D.D.&L. A.D.S.S./Forms/C.2118. ammunition. tracks left behind at POIX to follow	Major &?? Dickson

D.A.G.,
    3rd Echelon.

    Herewith War Diary for months of
April & May 1918.
    Delay in forwarding same is much
regretted.

26/6/18

                                  Major, D.A.D.O.S.
                                  24th Division.

WAR DIARY or INTELLIGENCE SUMMARY

Army Form C. 2118.

War Diary of 9th Div. M.T. Coy — April & May

Vol 31 32

A.A.S.O.S. 9th Division

Place	Date	Hour	Summary of Events and Information	Remarks and references to Appendices
COTTENCHY	1.4.18 to 3.4.18		April 1918. Division still in COTTENCHY where H.Q.Staff 9th Div A.O.D. Store was kept with office. Most of the demands were for technical parts of guns & machine guns magazines etc. Gun Park still at POIX. A long way to have to run back for stores – but this was necessary owing to question as to where the enemy were going to be stopped. During this period B. Warrant Officers were kept as much as possible in touch with their projects who were lying very close by. Railhead was at ST ROCHE. Most of this period (This is near AMIENS, outlying station Jns) 9th Div HQ also in this village. One portion of this was being	
BOVES	4.4.18		Moved to BOVES – Bivouac on arrival – Went to ABBEVILLE (No 8 Depot) for a few stores specially required such as 'Groundsheets' 'puttees' & boots. These were obtained from Armee reserve store was kept in Station yard at ST ROCHE for clothing & a few important stores. Division had been in fight up to now. French were farmers taken, no more of his three recoupings such villages as COTTENCHY proper requiring BOVES too. Heard that Division might be coming out altogether for a refit. When this was to be known not yet determined. Left BOVES for BOUTILLERIE same night about 12pm (Yes)	

WAR DIARY
INTELLIGENCE SUMMARY

Army Form C. 2118.

Place	Date	Hour	Summary of Events and Information	Remarks and references to Appendices
			A.D.O.S. 24th Division	
BOUTILLERIE	5.4.18		April 1918 (continued) Spent one night - kays have been for new transports, kit etc. Has an office in the village. Head definitely. Division were moving back right out to rest front. It was known at this period that enormous demands for nearly everything, with the coming of [?] from the Division. Brigades were told not to submit demands until they had had inspection completed, in the first few days arrival in new area - Written Asst. who had not been given the beginning of the arrival. ST VALERY was found to be nearly the centre of the new + So a large estimate demand was despatched today to HAVRE & ROUEN (for clothing). This was done to make sure of having some stores at once for the clamouring units in rest area. Lorries had been sent in overnight + they arrived about midday at ST VALERY. A good large store was found some night toffice. Four extra lorries were obtained from Division in the area. was lent nearly everything, would have to be sent out to Brigades. Obtained the exclusive use of three cars from Q much to the disgust of the A.A.Q.M.G. Summers did not come out with the Division. (WD)	
ST VALERY	6.4.18		Visited all Infantry Battalion offthew demands after their inspection to ascertain most of these back to my office same day. Blankets has been demanded in scale of 1 per man for whole of the Infantry who has lost all. These were drawn by ATD from LE TREPORT (about 10,000) deliveries to units within the day. (WD)	
	7.4.18			

WAR DIARY
INTELLIGENCE SUMMARY.

Army Form C. 2118.

Place	Date	Hour	Summary of Events and Information	Remarks and references to Appendices
ST VALERY	8.4.18		April 1918 (continued) ADMS 24th Division	

17IB were situated round CAYEUX with this Brn as Brigade H.Q.
LANCHÈRES was used as Brigade Ordnance dump from which place in this section were issued. 18IBF were also in this village.
72ⁿᵈ IB were at ARREST for H.Q. & as this was fairly central it was used for the Brigade A.O.D. dump. 73ʳᵈ IB were at FRIVILLE where this A.O.D. dump was situated. Stores were now arriving fast & it rained from 8 to in i.e. his up those that had broken up in man[oeuv]re trans; not actual units to Brigade dumps. Rosin & clothing began to arrive shortly afterwards & from all stores going out [rapidly] sometimes three times a day to each B. dump. This was satisfying to cleaning well. Of course there were a good many surprises between in view of the fact that there was no "Advanced A.O.D. Depots" except ABBEVILLE (not that it helped a lot) the system of estimates worked out pretty well. All that could be done.
By new demands were coming in & fact it was necessary to let off several for special demands regarding stores on which they have been intimates in the Base, who came up to scratch splendidly. Of course nearly all the units of this return was simplified by the fact that all were lost & thereupon help a certain amount was to come in by R.S.E. units etc which was landed in

WAR DIARY or INTELLIGENCE SUMMARY

Army Form C. 2118.

Place: ST VALERY
Date: 8.4.18 to 17.4.18
Summary of Events and Information: A.D.S. 74th Division

April 1918 (Continued)

Quiet to the station at ST VALERY where several tents (1 of the best) were kept up just beside the line to deal with any trouble. Private clothes, together with under old clothes, which was considerable. The position was rather accentuated by the fact that we expected to march any moment.

News was brought in saying that the Germans had moved out to SOREL almost 3½ kilos away, but ABBEVILLE in a motor car. They appeared to be getting very little satisfaction being administered under somewhat different systems by O.C. V Army Troops at LONGPRÉ. He has taken up from SALEUX at very short notice due to the much enquiring the area that no-string or places but then & thousands of troops together with small staff to administer them. He has 10 many troops under him by units direct without any Arty. representative being able to check to know whatever happens in matters. 5th Div artillery as far as A.D.) supply, was transferred afterwards and was known to 4 Army troops. I state form the Division to 5th — 58th Divisionaire D.A.D.S.

A. Corry, W.O. clerk Stenson, I two were left behind with Sgt. Saxton & two 24 Gunner.

Army Form C. 2118.

WAR DIARY
or
INTELLIGENCE SUMMARY.
(Erase heading not required.)

Instructions regarding War Diaries and Intelligence Summaries are contained in F. S. Regs., Part II. and the Staff Manual respectively. Title pages will be prepared in manuscript.

Place	Date	Hour	Summary of Events and Information	Remarks and references to Appendices
ST VALERY	8.4.18 to 17.4.18		April 1918 (continued) ADOS up to Division	

Consequently a train ambulance train it was obvious necessary they they try to take them under our wing. This was got well under way, as I am ADMS DDMS

Several trainloads of supplies starting from ST VALERY which they required. The fun Park had went to PONT REMY transfunction, between POIX & Kittens place with considerable success. Hence the R.A. Stores then from Lockers captured quickly.

Orders now came that the Division wants now into G.H.Q. reserve every 8th M was therefore made to complete the Two establish which this was done by running train not being lorries — to Shakespeare type transport here received from Base. After the Division Gnl up to near ST POL. Division HQ being at LA THIEULOYE, it was necessary to clear up for me any all the stores not required which has been kept at railhead. This was done & they were sent to ABBEVILLE

No 8 A.O.D. Depôt.
The move did cause a little from but we were here, to have had the 11 days that a certain amount not to them. & has the satisfaction them that G.H.Q. reserve should give me another port chance to finish than off. The personnel departs move up almost at same time to practically ST POL.

Lt LOVE Office joins for duty Instruction during this period which makes

Army Form C. 2118.

WAR DIARY
or
INTELLIGENCE SUMMARY.
(Erase heading not required.)

Instructions regarding War Diaries and Intelligence Summaries are contained in F. S. Regs., Part II. and the Staff Manual respectively. Title pages will be prepared in manuscript.

Place	Date	Hour	Summary of Events and Information	Remarks and references to Appendices
LA THIEULOYE	17.4.18 to 31.4.18		April (continued) 1918 A.D.S.T. 25th Div (Sir) Moved to LA THIEULOYE with tents leaving one WO behind to clear Travellers Rest everything left behind at ABBEVILLE. Find alter. in the new village mostly under Canvas with Stc tents & Marquees. Each armourer has been sent out to his Battalion during this period at ST VALERY. Fifth went on quite well here — The others were a little different to fix up owing to the trucks Horse Base has been for 24th Division head rest to LONGPRÉ & demand item by O.O. 2A Troops Spare were dealt; direct with the attached instead of to O.O. 4 E.A. Troops by Special arrangement, this would have for men was not the man interesting namely: one lorry undercarriage, the rural Comm. flame been that "As Advanced A.O.D. with depots should have been in existence as the composition was from the company under various circumstances demands would be long. Some divisions only let 3 days to refit in. During this period Division has been in 18thCorps. The present railhead is DIEVAL this work may depend on amount normal again. Proper days for bulk demands being worked to one more... J.H.Skevald. Major AADSD 25th Div now.	

Army Form C. 2118.

WAR DIARY
or
INTELLIGENCE SUMMARY.

(Erase heading not required.)

Instructions regarding War Diaries and Intelligence Summaries are contained in F. S. Regs., Part II. and the Staff Manual respectively. Title pages will be prepared in manuscript.

D.A.D.O.S. 74th Division

Place	Date	Hour	Summary of Events and Information	Remarks and references to Appendices
LA THIEULOYE	1.5.18 to 3.5.18		May 1918. Stores are coming up quite well from Calais Base — Save difficulty in obtaining Artillery Technical stores which HAVRE could not supply. This was afterwards found to be due to the fact that the latter Base did not transfer the own but Calais. Certain stores, there are two or three other man numbers of importance required articles, had to be obtained by lorry direct from No 8 B.O.D. at ABBEVILLE. R.A. men are attempting to the area round LE CAUROY (S.E. of ST POL). HQ. R.A. was here. A marquee was pitched for tall stores sent to this point where a N.C.O. Storeman & Clerk were left to deal entirely with R.A. One lorry took stores nearly daily.	(R.)
BOYEFFLES	4.5.18 to 8.5.18		Division moved up into the line (VIMY sector) taking over from the 3rd Canadian Division — Div: H.Q. going into SAINS EN GOHELLE. Ordnance stores taken over from Canadians. This is an old Ammunition Dump together with a little fintage made quite a good store trophies. Railhead was at BARLIN-JOUY.	
GOUY SERVINS	9.5.18 to 31.5.18		Owing to shortage of space in way of accommodation it was decided that Rear Divisional H.O. should move to GOUY SERVINS which place restore of A & Q Staff moved. At this place was much nearer to R.A., in order to keep in touch with Q Branch.	

WAR DIARY
or
INTELLIGENCE SUMMARY.
(Erase heading not required.)

Army Form C. 2118.

Place	Date	Hour	Summary of Events and Information	Remarks and references to Appendices
GOUY SERVINS W5 central Map 44 b	9.5.18 (cont'd) to 31.5.18		May 1918 (continued) — ADSS up to Division + to keep fire from the enemy's shelling need to a clear field of fire between GOUY SERVINS & MAISIL BOUCHE. An extra Lewin depot between GOUY SERVINS & MAISIL BOUCHE — Stores being sent to BOYEFFLES was formed. Stores being sent to BOYEFFLES as afternoon dumps by lorry each day, R.A. Several of the small units come under train stores. Capt enquiry that light Railway should be used. This was arranged — two platinum have to be sent as countrymen to rail trucks — two platinum — two platinum have to be sent as countrymen to rail trucks up to BOYEFFLES siding. There two men are required as the train is often pulled out in two parts & A.O.D. Stores thus separated. There is often a great delay in the light rail stores taken many hours for too small a distance. Local bottom of A.Aircraft mountain trains to 17th VB. Front is very quiet — nothing beyond the ordinary routine to report. — Weather extremely hot. Certain stores which are considered the only certainty to DS Bats. during active operations. Being enumerated & prepare for withdrawal to Divisional stores were in rear.	

S.B. Stevens
Major ADSS 2d Division

Army Form C. 2118.

D.A.D.O.S
24 Div

WAR DIARY
or
INTELLIGENCE SUMMARY.
(Erase heading not required.)

Summary of Events and Information DADOS 24th Div:

VII 33

Place	Date	Hour	Summary of Events and Information	Remarks and references to Appendices
GOUY SERVINS W5 Central Map 44 b	1.6.18 to 15.6.18		On leave - DADOS 72nd Division acted for this period. A simple type of Aircraft Lewis Mounting was made & sent to 72nd Brigade of Infantry. This is made out of two lengths of duckboard & a foot of round iron. As a temporary measure, until anything better is thought out it is a very useful substitute - Everything quite normal & stores coming up well from the Base.	
	16.6.18 to 23.6.18		ADOS visited Divn. Extra Lewis guns issued to each Battalion bringing Battalions to 32 f/pltn. Guns sent to for Anti Air Craft. At these Guns have to be emptied guns lkg in Bn. Ammunition Mags to them are not fit to have until they have been tested at the Visited two Brigades of 59th Div Artillery attached. 295th + 296th Tarrangement to have both to send in to their SMC. One Lip of each Brain & Stc. complete (two R.A.T. Section) also attached to Corps field Cashier for departmental pay - Divns Staff Captain 59th Division R.A. who have been attached for A.O.D. Services. Men to advance upon Boot-stores on demand there daily. Took an Armourer & Iron back for duty on this Jackson Rifle for a fortnight. First 4 cars of new kind of Suitcases in the detachment. As sent to 24 Div Ammunition Stay MD	
	24.6.18			

Army Form C. 2118.

WAR DIARY
or
INTELLIGENCE SUMMARY.
(Erase heading not required.)

June 1918 (continued)   D.A.D.S. 24th Division

Place	Date	Hour	Summary of Events and Information	Remarks and references to Appendices
GOUY SERVINS (Map) 44 B W 5 Central	25-6-18		Two Warrant Officers have arrived to replace with the new kind of Influenza now prevalent in this Division. This is making Staff very shorthanded. Stars to refill this point in mown. Weather the & Champagne. Weather very cold.	J.M.D.
	26-6-18		One probe per lorries. Hitchins gun been withdrawn till now instead - 6 chaff cutter received for issue when to Division - 3 to Town Majors for this area. To GAMACHE also DIEPPE for local purchase fitting of 2 bbls which could not promptly be completed owing to the proprietor having had to evacuate AMIENS take up this business in new town.	J.M.D. J.M.D. J.M.D.
	27-6-18		Stores up today from Base. 59th Division drawing very heavily on paint. They are now in reserve & are anxious that all their vehicles painted up. Monthly statement of bulk issues sent out. Must better figures - Proposed to start a new system of limiting bulk issues of certain items to a limited figure per cent both in case of horses & men - giving units a three month account during which period they can draw any part of the figures laid down. An Special applications for larger figures are to be sent to Divisional Q. Staff.	
	28-6-18		Certain items such as Respirators arrives, withdrawn from H.Q. unit, as a limit.	J.M.D.

WAR DIARY
or
INTELLIGENCE SUMMARY.

Army Form C. 2118.

Place	Date	Hour	Summary of Events and Information	Remarks and references to Appendices
GOUY SERVINS	June 1918 (continued)		ADS 94th Division	
	29.6.18		A.D.O.S. called also S.O.C. Chief Clerk down with this new complaint (type of Influenza). Horse shoes thicknesses sent out to relieving Point. It is understood that 59th Divisional Artillery attached are the mares shortly to II Corps. O.C. Machine Gun Battalion has been asked have all his Lewis Guns fitted with a copper collar sweated on behind the union on the tube. Weather fine.	JHT
	30.6.18		Have emplacement of Horse Shoes north for 59th Div Artillery at Railhead (SAVY) together with several other bulk stores up to 2 army loads. Information seems that 59th Div Artillery are definitely to return to 61st Division. Acc. personnel despatched today to 61st Divisional ADS with no lorry petrol ahead seems to that formation. The balance up at brass dump Railhead has been reconsigned to II VION R.H. the presence up to 59th Div Ammu from this this Point. (MD). Preparing to move Mobile Vet to SAINS EN GOHELLE to be completed by 2nd July, using BOYEFFLES Sidings in DECAUVILLE Rail again. To prospect actual position of Officer etc	

J.H.Tennant
Major A.D.V.S. 24th Division

D.A.D.O.S.
24th
DIVISION.

No. ....
Date ....

DHQ
24th Division

Herewith my war
Diary for the month
of July — Delay
is regretted — (away on a course)

J.H.D.Sheppard

WAR DIARY
or
INTELLIGENCE SUMMARY

Army Form C. 2118.

Vol 34

Place	Date	Hour	Summary of Events and Information	Remarks and references to Appendices
	July 1918		A.D.M.S. 74th Division	
	1.7.18		Stove placed in a small hut at Govt Station. These are the particulars ones recently returned by units such as respirators etc to be secured temporary arrangement for the Division.	
	2.7.18		Question of moving sick etc back to SAINS not reconsidered. Many of the blankets (over 3000) issued for the new Influenza trouble are now coming back to store. No further definite advice to Divisions Rear HQ move back to SAINS.	
	3.7.18		Three Lewis Machine Guns received from Corps Troops. Arrangers to change w/ serviceable clothing some on the spot. Serviceable requisite buyer must to OC 73 Amber Buffalo Carts where it can be better looked after. Stores received from Rushfiers.	
	4.7.18		Two Brigade Warrant Officers have summons returned to duty from Base Hospital after having this new Influenza which now seems to be dying out. Four Lewis Machine Guns were finally received from to Divisional Armament Coy.	
	5.7.18 6.7.18		To BOULOGNE for local purchase; obtained Klaxon Horn for Speaker P.S. & some particular flags for the D.C.	

Army Form C. 2118.

WAR DIARY
or
INTELLIGENCE SUMMARY.
(Erase heading not required.)

Place	Date	Hour	Summary of Events and Information	Remarks and references to Appendices
GOUY SERVINS	7.7.18		Store up from rail head. Inspected a few of the at Gouy Station which has had all the unit supplies A.O.J. Stores put in for safety. There cannot matter of any spindles & box periscopes. The former are used by very few units in the Division as the men are not trained sufficiently in their use to make them sufficiently useful. The Box periscopes sent in are about 25% of the figure allowed in G.1098 - Just issue of cycles made since the March German Offensive - Thirty two advised as being on rail.	A.A.D.S. 7th Division
	8.7.18		Store up at railhead. A.D.O.S. Cavalry Corps visited the detachment & presented the A.O.C. units. Service by the D.O.S.	
	9.7.18 to 12.7.18		At present the Corps Commander is making a war on vehicles, especially Cookers & Water Carts. It is found that many units are not in possession of their correct spares for these vehicles & also seem extraordinary vague about the parts they should have demanded to make them complete - In many cases they have not their inventories -	J.A.M.

Army Form C. 2118.

WAR DIARY
or
INTELLIGENCE SUMMARY.
(Erase heading not required.)

Instructions regarding War Diaries and Intelligence Summaries are contained in F. S. Regs., Part II. and the Staff Manual respectively. Title pages will be prepared in manuscript.

A.D.S.T./24th Division

Place	Date	Hour	Summary of Events and Information	Remarks and references to Appendices
GOUY SERVINS	13.7.18 & 14.7.18		July 1918 (continued) A.D.S.T. visited A.S.H.Q. New system of fixing a maximum Bulk Stock programme per cent men & animals is being tried from 20th July. The account will be a three monthly one when any credit balance elapses. No more than 14 days allowance to be drawn at any one time (except for small units where, acting on this, do not exceed the amount 3 months allowance, per diem). Refits become a special case (apply for any week) other cause for an an unproportionate demand is to be referred to Q Branch for authority. The figures are based on a six month summer & winter scale for the Division less a small percentage. A comparative statement of understandings will be published every 3 months.	
BOYEFFLES	15.7.18		Motored down to BOYEFFLES - Men under canvas - Same railhead for horse camp & light rail. Reserve store stuff left at GOUY -	(MSO)
	16.7.18		A.D.S.T. called. Visited D.O.T. office reference Ordnance Convoi.	(MSO)
	17.7.18		150 Special Anti Yellow Cross Gas Combination Suits received for issue among the infantry.	(MSO) (MSO)

Army Form C. 2118.

WAR DIARY
or
INTELLIGENCE SUMMARY.
(Erase heading not required.)

Instructions regarding War Diaries and Intelligence Summaries are contained in F. S. Regs., Part II. and the Staff Manual respectively. Title pages will be prepared in manuscript.

Place	Date	Hour	Summary of Events and Information	Remarks and references to Appendices
BOYEFFLES	18.7.18 to 22.7.18		July 19th (continued) from A.D.O.S. 24th Division. Radium Dial Sights are being issued to the Artillery in exchange for old inoperative Sights. All the outstanding demands for cycles have now been met. Treated again fair with occasional bursts of thundery downpour. Three Cookers are being prepared for Boxpatra in every detail as specimens for units to model from that they make be repaired for the various shows that are now going on. No. 19 Ordnance Depot for a 14 days Ammunition Course.	

J.M. Shepherd
Major S.A.D.O.S. 24th Division

14 | Aug Sep Oct | Army Form C. 2118.

WAR DIARY
or
INTELLIGENCE SUMMARY.
(Erase heading not required.)

A.D.S. 94th Division

Place	Date	Hour	Summary of Events and Information	Remarks and references to Appendices
	August 1918			
BOYEFFLES	13.8.18 to 17.8.18		Returns for Ammunition Course. Division kept denuded of horse flesh — heaters very poor — nights perfectly clear, much bombing. Railhead changed to BARLIN. Great difficulty in obtaining soap from Base. Certain amount purchased. Prices high. Spotted dial sights have now been issued to 17 Can: F.A. A.D.S. visited stores.	37 38
	18.8.18 to 24.8.18		Stores coming up to Railhead quite regular, demands being met by base mill. MAJOR McGOWAN took over on duties whilst I left for leave to Paris.	

J. M. Stewart
Major
A.D.S. 94th Division

WAR DIARY
or
INTELLIGENCE SUMMARY.

Army Form C. 2118.

Place	Date	Hour	Summary of Events and Information	Remarks and references to Appendices
BOYEFFLES	1.9.18 to 20.9.18		September 1918. Returned from leave. This chief clerk (Conductor Healy) extremely seedy. Hands over duties to fit Conductor Frogg. Conductor Healy too of duty after his can thought to be left for a C.C.S. with his orders to proceed to England on becoming fit again. Weather very wet. The accommodation in tents becoming difficult. Mr. Persistre (Sub Conductor) joined to replace Cpl. Colpitts Healy. He has had no experience of Divisional Ordnance duties in France. Applies for Sub Conductor Goody to be Chief Clerk. His position as Acting Conductor was soon agreed upon by D.O.S. He was taken that rank. The issue of Gas Respirators very high in this section. Issues have been very heavy.	S.A.D.O.S. 46th Division. 1st
21.9.18 to 29.9.18		All preparations for a large operation being prepared. A large quantity of special stores required by the Division. These were obtained after the issue had reported to Army the magnitude of the demand. - Time of Indents	
30.9.18		Not permit of the long round about official channel of the stores are to be available. Division moving up off the live track to rest at LOCHEUX. J.H. Thomas Major S.A.D.O.S. 46 Division	1st

Army Form C. 2118.

WAR DIARY
or
INTELLIGENCE SUMMARY.
(Erase heading not required.)

BA 205 24th Division

Place	Date	Hour	Summary of Events and Information	Remarks and references to Appendices
LUCHEUX	1·X·18		October 1918 Officers settled down in LUCHEUX – All demands now transfers to Havre & Rouen which always seems to cause delay. A reserve store had fortunately been formed from which it was possible to keep the Division supplied with the essentials. Demands for winter clothing were already made out from units on Strength. Dress returns &c to reach Bras by 15/X/18 as per SRO. One returned so far has only been authorised for men Driven Div. in S.H.Q. rooms. 3" Stokes mortars have been fitted with Lewis Lambs or Dix. Ammn. Wagons to keep a man carriage. We need the piece which at a hinds this. Two Mobile carriages to be issued to each Newton Major. There were afterwards authorised to be drawn from certain places but were never ready. Note with action in all Infantry Btns to November after the trans whole were herded the BGOs were carefully ordered just Division moved up into line a little east of NOEUVRES. Stores were	
MOEUVRES	6·X·18 to 8·X·18		moved up & dump of 59th Divisional Ordnance was taken over together with a good quantity Stokes stores	

14

WAR DIARY
or
INTELLIGENCE SUMMARY.
(Erase heading not required.)

Army Form C. 2118.

ASST. DY. HD Division

Place	Date	Hour	Summary of Events and Information	Remarks and references to Appendices
FONTAINE NOTRE DAMES	9.10.18 to 12.10.18		October 1918 (continued) Moved up to FONTAINE. Division attacking South of CAMBRAI. Few stores required only essentials such as guns, rifle oil, flannelette, box respirators. On account of Signals being in touch with Q Branch every endeavour being made to keep at same location as D.H.Q (rear)	
B.20.d. (51 A)	13.10.18 to 16.10.18		Moved again to this location on the LE CATEAU road. Stores gradually being collected to units cannot take them while moving. Advanced from Park at SUMMIT SIDING getting very much out of range — to CAMBRAI. BAPAUME road being in terrible condition. Railhead has been at FAUX VAUCRICOURT. Tied now up to MARCOING. Stores still growing. Funds taken liberally. Corps state that cattle loses the heaviest Division. This means a great deal of transport. Winter Clothing also has begun to arrive. Practically no stove pipes being saved except a few for officers changers. Division still pushing on further, around HAUSSY.	
AVESNES LES AUBERT	17.10.18 to 21.10.18		Moved up to AVESNES. Really good place. Bulk of stores left behind at B.20.b & only essentials taken up at first. Stores taken over contained an enormous quantity of German stores of every description. As many of these as possible were sent back in empty lorries to Railhead for despatch to the Base	

Army Form C. 2118.

WAR DIARY
or
INTELLIGENCE SUMMARY.
(Erase heading not required.)

Instructions regarding War Diaries and Intelligence Summaries are contained in F. S. Regs., Part II. and the Staff Manual respectively. Title pages will be prepared in manuscript.

Place	Date	Hour	Summary of Events and Information	Remarks and references to Appendices
			October 1918 (Continued)	Stated by Divisions
CAMBRAI	22.X.18 to 26.X.18		Winter clothing has not yet been received, the general delay in railway, due to enemy to line wanted in trucks being very late toward one. Moved back to CAMBRAI whilst division was relieved by 19th Division. A certain amount of winter clothing was issued here but of quite demand but priority. Roses were met the priority outstanding since 6/X/18 + have not allowed when winning them on this account. Steam action afterwards hosts to but the role of the Divisional Point of repairing shops out of steam due to shortage of material. British mass baths into line took over by degrees from 5th Division.	MD MO MO
ST AUBERT	27.X.18 to 31.X.18		Railheads now moved up to CAMBRAI ANNEXE. She was moved up to ST AUBERT + All personnel except booksop which remains helds at B.20.b to function. Also look after the bath of the Battn Hors which had been left behind. Here we can Henceforth be required later. Units drawing a certain quantity of Hors, but owing to the possibility of moving again many Units they had declined they would tend not to take. One of the substantion difficulties has been the replacement of vehicles. It may frequently happens were done by the unit had to wait whilst the were replaced by Hors (which we gave, Present establishment allows 10 to 16 Days. J.H.A. Stretton Major	

A.D.S.S./Forms/C. 2118.

WAR DIARY or INTELLIGENCE SUMMARY

Army Form C. 2118.

Vol 38

Place	Date	Hour	Summary of Events and Information	Remarks and references to Appendices
			Staff 74th Division	
ST AUBERT	1.XI.18 & 2.XI.18		November 1918. Owing especially to the train transportation difficulty being experienced with transport, the distance to railhead.	
BERMERAIN	3.XI.18 & 4.XI.18		Moved on to BERMERAIN taking store formed as far as possible. Received gear at CAMBRAI. ROUEN owing considerable trouble - clearly stated fact that matters have been outstanding since 6/X/18, was in a definite truck - on arrival no further was found at all.	not
WARMIES LE GRAND	5.XI.18 6		Railhead moved up to AUBERT - Lorries ful bring stores Railhead ST AUBERT + BERMERAIN stores up to new one at WARMIES LE GRAND - Divn was should	
	9.XI.18		Divisional H.Q. in same place first Considerably for the first night or so - Lorries drawing very little & consequently the stores are growing thin. Railhead SOLESMES -	not
BAVAY	10.XI.18		Moved up to BAVAY - Considerable difficulties with transport owing due to minus & bridges & trains broken - This applies especially to lorries -	not
	11.XI.18		Division HQ moved just outside the town to allow 7 Corps HQ in - Division coming out of the line would BAVAY to get up to strength do what repairing is necessary Lorries Clearing dump at ST AUBERT up to the Railhead SOLESMES - Armistice Signed for 11 A.M. today -	not

Army Form C. 2118.

WAR DIARY
or
INTELLIGENCE SUMMARY.
(Erase heading not required.)

Instructions regarding War Diaries and Intelligence
Summaries are contained in F. S. Regs., Part II.
and the Staff Manual respectively. Title pages
will be prepared in manuscript.

Place	Date	Hour	Summary of Events and Information	Remarks and references to Appendices
BAVAY	13.XI.18		November 1918 (continued) Units now collecting stores well. Approx. 60 tons available being the allowance of demands for things which they can not take on into the balance of all dumps being brought up to BRAY. Railhead after SOLESMES. All battle stores being despatched there. Cloth being asked for – further harm Army state the only have articles of special equipment may be passed there first and that Divisions must hold all stores in indication till true required complete scale.	Stores to Divisions
14.XI.18 & 15.XI.18		Units have been made up in clothing & all expendable stores for winter comforts. A move is shortly expected back to Corps locator which is not yet settled – Division is not going into Germany to present –	
16.XI.18 to 18.XI.18		Railhead still SOLESMES. Alot of units returning large quantities of Clothing etc. Owing to the great distance from railhead the use of a dozen empty returning supply lorries has been used – Granted a month's leave. The Adjutant of the train is acting for me as there are no Ordnance Officers available by the time.	J.H.S.Neptone? Major & ADO 2e Division

A.D.S.S./Forms/C. 2118.

Army Form C. 2118.

24

WAR DIARY
or
INTELLIGENCE SUMMARY.
(Erase heading not required.)

Wt. 39

STAP 24th Division

Place	Date	Hour	Summary of Events and Information	Remarks and references to Appendices
TOURNAI	23.12.18 to 31.12.18		Returned from leave to find the Division has moved to TOURNAI & has so far as Ordnance Services are concerned got a lot of unit, attached such as R.A.F. Labour Coys. Railhead is close twenty kilos - the time taken for trucks to come sometimes as much as 5 days. 72 I.B. is in the town, while 73rd is only 5 kilos out so that they can be to draw stores. The 17th is half way out to Lille & consequently stores have to be run out to them. The R.A. & other units are close hand. The A.D.O.S. has been over several times. Two guns have been withdrawn per Battery R.F.A. & all personnel No 9 are now to be withdrawn.	

J.H. Sherman
Major D.A.D.O.S. 24 Division

to 24th Division
to Division
first

www.ingramcontent.com/pod-product-compliance
Lightning Source LLC
Chambersburg PA
CBHW081542160426
43191CB00011B/1822